SALVATION BY GRACE

Colin Dye

Sovereign World

Sovereign World Ltd
PO Box 777
Tonbridge
Kent TN11 0ZS
England

Copyright © 1999 by Colin Dye

All rights reserved. No part of this publication may be reproduced, stored in a retrieval system or transmitted, in any form or by any means, electronic, mechanical, photocopying or otherwise, without the prior written consent of the publisher. Except that, the activity material at the rear of the book may be photocopied by purchasers to use in a small group under their leadership.

Scriptural quotations are from the New King James Version, Thomas Nelson Inc., 1991.

ISBN 1 85240 213 X

Typeset by CRB Associates, Reepham, Norfolk
Printed in England by Clays Ltd, St Ives plc.

FOREWORD

The material in this *Sword of the Spirit* series has been developed over the past ten years at Kensington Temple in London as we have sought to train leaders for the hundreds of churches and groups we have established. Much of the material was initially prepared for the students who attend the International Bible Institute of London – which is based at our church.

Over the years, other churches and colleges have asked if they may use some of our material to help them establish training courses for leaders in their towns and countries. This series has been put together partly to meet this growing need, as churches everywhere seek to train large numbers of new leaders to serve the growth that God is giving.

The material has been constantly refined – by myself, by the students as they have responded, by my many associate pastors, and by the staff at the Bible Institute. In particular, my colleague Timothy Pain has been responsible for sharpening, developing and shaping my different courses and notes into this coherent series.

I hope that many people will use this series in association with our developing Satellite Bible School, but I also pray that churches around the world will use the books to train leaders.

We live at a time when increasing numbers of new churches are being started, and I am sure that we will see even more startling growth in the next few decades. It is vital that we re-examine the way we train and release leaders so that these new churches have the best possible biblical foundation. This series is our contribution to equipping tomorrow's leaders with the eternal truths that they need.

Colin Dye

CONTENTS

Introduction		7
Part One	Holiness, Sin and Forgiveness	9
Part Two	Self-consistency	21
Part Three	Substitution and Sacrifice	31
Part Four	Covenants of Grace	49
Part Five	Salvation and Atonement	61
Part Six	Salvation and Revelation	73
Part Seven	Salvation and Victory	85
Part Eight	Salvation and New Life	101
Part Nine	By Grace through Faith	115
Activities for individuals and small groups		131

INTRODUCTION

The little word 'save' is one of the commonest verbs in the English language. Every day, we all use it dozens of times in association with words like time, money, goals, fuel, animals, stamps, paper, inner cities, computer work, derelict buildings, drowning people, and so on.

But even though we use 'save' in an amazingly wide variety of contexts, its general meaning is clear. To save something means to preserve it, to rescue it, to reclaim it, to deliver it from danger or to prevent it from falling into misuse.

When it comes to Christianity, however, the meaning of 'save' can seem less clear. Although most believers understand that 'being saved' means being preserved, rescued, reclaimed, delivered and resuscitated, many are not sure *how* this happens, *why* it happens, and *what* its consequences are in human life.

The basic idea of salvation is easy to grasp: *God* finds the lost, gives new life to the dead, cleanses the dirty, forgives the guilty, turns the defeated into victors, releases the imprisoned, and so on. But the *why*, *how* and *so what* of salvation involve some very hard thinking.

New believers instinctively know what the simple word 'to save' means, but they soon realise that a host of technical words are associated with 'being saved'. Many are bewildered until somebody explains the differences between, for example, atonement, covenant, election, glorification, judgement, justification, predestination, propitiation, redemption, regeneration, sanctification, and so on.

Although these technical words can confuse believers, the important ideas behind them shape the way that we think about salvation, the way that we experience salvation, and the way that we reach out to others with the good news of salvation.

If we do not work hard to grasp the full biblical *why*, *how* and *so what* of salvation, we are bound to move away from the totally God-focused view of biblical salvation and to start to think and speak about it in an unhelpful human-centred way.

This is a book for believers who are eager to study God's Word to learn about salvation, and are keen to discover God's revelation about the purpose and nature of Christ's death, the means by which it is made effective, and the results of his death in human life.

Please ensure that you read all the references – and tick the margin boxes as you go along to show that you have. Answer every question and think through each point as it is made. Before moving on to a new section, think carefully about the implications of what you have studied. Please allow God to speak to you as you study his word.

At the end of the book, there is some activity material and questions. Please make sure that you study Parts 1–9 before beginning to work through the activities, as this will ensure that you have an overview of the biblical teaching about salvation before you try to apply the details of any one aspect. These questions will help you to grasp and apply the scriptural material that you have studied.

You will also be able to use the activity pages when you teach the material to small groups. Please feel free to photocopy these pages and distribute them to any group you are leading. Although you should work through all the questions when you are studying on your own, please don't expect a small group to cover all the material.

By the time you finish this book, it is my prayer that you will have a far better understanding of fallen human nature, of the wonderful person and work of Christ, and of the way that the cross dominates and unites the whole Bible from Genesis to Revelation.

Even more than this, I pray that you will be overwhelmed by the infinite grace of God, which has worked in salvation at so much cost; and that you will respond to this grace by living out your salvation in such a way that you draw others to his grace for themselves.

Colin Dye

PART ONE

holiness, sin and forgiveness

Jesus' famous story about a lost son, in Luke 15:11–32, illustrates the heavenly Father's unconditional grace in saving undeserving sinners.

In the parable, the son's repentance was not a pre-condition of his father's gracious love, it was the means which enabled him to receive his father's forgiveness. The father was looking and waiting long before his son returned home; and, as soon as he saw his son, he rushed out to welcome him with passionate, generous joy – without a question about his motives or misdeeds.

The parable is such a gripping celebration of 'divine grace at work in human salvation' that it prompts some people to ask why the heavenly Father does not forgive us in much the same way – without any need for the cross. They do not understand why divine forgiveness depends on Christ's death, and so they wonder why God does not forgive us – like the father in the parable – without a costly sacrifice.

But people who think like this have not grasped either the seriousness of human sin or the holiness of God; they have not appreciated the scale of the confrontation between human rebellion

Luke 15:11–32

and divine perfection. In fact, the Bible implies that human sin is an immovable object which is faced with the irresistible force of God's holy wrath.

This means that there is a harder question to ask about salvation than 'Why does God need the cross to forgive us?' The most difficult issue to resolve can be considered from two sides:

- *How can God show his love in forgiving sinners without destroying his holiness?*

- *And, how can God show his holiness in punishing sin without abandoning his love?*

HUMAN SIN

The New Testament uses four main Greek words for sin. Although these are largely synonymous, they carry slightly different shades of meaning which help us to understand the subtle and complex nature of sin. All the words convey the idea of failing to match God's perfect standard, and they describe deeds and attitudes which separate us from each other and from God.

Hamartia

Hamartia is the most common word for sin. It is sometimes used for outer sinful acts, but more commonly describes the inner state of sinfulness. It is the irresistible inner moral power which controls us.

Hamartia depicts sin as missing a target and failing to attain a goal. It points to both inner disobedience which cannot say 'yes' to God and outer nonconformity to his standards. These deeply affect our relationship with the holy God; until all our *hamartia* is removed, we are eternally alienated from him.

Hamartia is used, for example, in Matthew 12:31; John 8:21, 34, 46; 9:41; 15:22–24; 19:11; Acts 7:60; Romans 3:9; 5:12–13, 20–21; 6:1–6, 12–17; 7:7–25; 8:2–3; 1 Corinthians 15:56; Hebrews 3:13; 9:26; 10:6–8; 11:25; 12:4; 13:11; James 1:15; 2:9; 4:17; 5:15, 20; 1 John 1:7–8; 3:4–9 and 5:16.

Matthew 12:31 ☐
John 8:21, 34, 46 ☐
    9:41 ☐
    15:22–24 ☐
    19:11 ☐
Acts 7:60 ☐
Romans 3:9 ☐
    5:12–13 ☐
    5:20–21 ☐
    6:1–6 ☐
    6:12–17 ☐
    7:7–25 ☐
    8:2–3 ☐
1 Corinthians
    15:56 ☐
Hebrews 3:13 ☐
    9:26 ☐
    10:6–8 ☐
    11:25 ☐
    12:4 ☐
    13:11 ☐
James 1:15 ☐
    2:9 ☐
    4:17 ☐
    5:15, 20 ☐
1 John 1:7–8 ☐
    3:4–9 ☐
    5:16 ☐

Paraptoma

Most Bible versions translate *paraptoma* as 'trespass' or 'offence'. This means a false step or blunder, a falling away from what is true and right. *Paraptoma* emphasises the thoughtless, careless nature of sin.

Paraptoma is used, for example, in Matthew 6:14–15; 18:35; Mark 11:25–26; Romans 4:25; 5:15–20; 11:11–12; 2 Corinthians 5:19; Galatians 6:1; Ephesians 1:7; 2:1, 5; Colossians 2:13 and James 5:16.

Parabasis

Parabasis stresses the wilful, deliberate side of sin. It means overstepping rather than stumbling, and is a deliberate deviation from the true path, a pre-meditated breaking of the law. It is translated as 'transgression' in most versions of the Bible.

Parabasis is used in, for example, Romans 2:23; 4:15; 5:13–14, 20; 7:7, 13; Galatians 3:19; 1 Timothy 2:14 and Hebrews 2:2; 9:15.

Anomia

Anomia means lawlessness, wickedness or iniquity, and refers to the opposite of whatever is right and good. It is used in 2 Thessalonians 2:3 to show that lawless iniquity is the opposite of God.

Anomia is used in Matthew 7:23; 13:41; 23:28; 24:12; Romans 4:7; 6:19; 2 Corinthians 6:14; 2 Thessalonians 2:7; Titus 2:14; Hebrews 1:9; 10:17 and 1 John 3:4.

Other words

The New Testament occasionally uses some other Greek words to describe particular facets of sin. For example:

- *adikia*; unrighteousness, or not being right – Luke 13:27; 16:8; 18:6; Acts 1:18; 8:23; 2 Timothy 2:19 and James 3:6.

- *adikema*; an iniquity, misdeed or wrong-doing – Acts 18:14; 24:20 and Revelation 18:5.

- *poneria*; a terrible wickedness – Matthew 22:18; Mark 7:22; Luke 11:39; Romans 1:29 and 1 Corinthians 5:8.

Matthew 6:14–15 ☐
18:35 ☐
Mark 11:25–26 ☐
Romans 4:25 ☐
5:15–20 ☐
11:11–12 ☐
2 Corinthians 5:19 ☐
Galatians 6:1 ☐
Ephesians 1:7 ☐
2:1, 5 ☐
Colossians 2:13 ☐
James 5:16 ☐
Romans 2:23 ☐
4:15 ☐
5:13–20 ☐
7:7, 13 ☐
Galatians 3:19 ☐
1 Timothy 2:14 ☐
Hebrews 2:2 ☐
9:15 ☐
Matthew 7:23 ☐
13:41 ☐
23:28 ☐
24:12 ☐
Romans 4:7 ☐
6:19 ☐
2 Corinthians 6:14 ☐
2 Thessalonians 2:3, 7 ☐
Titus 2:14 ☐
Hebrews 1:9 ☐
10:17 ☐
1 John 3:4 ☐
Luke 13:27 ☐
16:8 ☐
18:6 ☐
Acts 1:18 ☐
8:23 ☐
2 Timothy 2:19 ☐
James 3:6 ☐
Acts 18:14 ☐
24:20 ☐
Revelation 18:5 ☐
Matthew 22:18 ☐
Mark 7:22 ☐
Luke 11:39 ☐
Romans 1:29 ☐
1 Corinthians 5:8 ☐

- *paranomia*; law-breaking – 2 Peter 2:16
- *opheilema*; indebtedness – Matthew 6:12; Romans 4:4
- *aition*; fault or crime – Luke 23:4, 14, 22; John 18:38; 19:4–6

Sin

All these Greek words imply an ideal – either an objective standard that we fail to match or a boundary which we cross deliberately or casually.

The Bible assumes that God established this ideal, and that his holy nature is itself the ideal – not some list of rules which are exterior to his being. As God made humanity in his image, his personal standard must also be our human standard. We see this in Romans 2:15.

The Bible teaches much about sin, and always stresses its extreme seriousness. It shows that sin is a failure to love God with all our being, and a refusal to acknowledge and obey him as Creator and Lord.

As created beings, men and women are essentially dependent on God. Sin, therefore, is an action and an attitude of independence or self-dependence. It is implicitly hostile to God as Creator and Lord, and is always essentially an active rebellion against *him*.

Many sinful actions may appear to hurt only those people who are affected by the deeds. For example, it might seem that David's sin with Bathseba, in 2 Samuel 11, was directed against Uriah and Michal. But sin primarily expresses our personal rebellion against God – this is the deep truth which David's confession recognises in Psalm 51:4.

The Bible develops this understanding of sin as essentially affecting God by showing that it is:

- *universal to all humanity* – Romans 1–3
- *both internal attitudes and external actions* – Romans 1:29–31; 13:13; 1 Corinthians 5:10–13; 6:9–10; 2 Corinthians 12:20–21; Galatians 5:19–21; Ephesians 4:31; 5:3–5; Colossians 3:5–8; 1 Timothy 1:9–10; 2 Timothy 3:2–3; Titus 3:3
- *enslavement to Satan, God's enemy* – 1 John 3:8–10
- *a slave-master* – Romans 6:16–17
- *rebellion against God* – Luke 15:11–32

- *alienation from God* – John 7:7; Romans 5:10; 1 John 2:16
- *unbelief in God* – John 5:24; 16:9
- *blindness and darkness towards God* – John 1:4–9; 8:12; 1 John 2:8–9
- *lawlessness* – Romans 6:19; 2 Corinthians 6:14; 1 John 3:4
- *indebtedness to God* – Matthew 6:12; Colossians 2:14
- *falsehood about God* – Romans 1:18, 25; Ephesians 4:25; 2 Thessalonians 2:11–12; 1 Timothy 6:5
- *deviation from God* – Romans 2:23
- *disobedience to God* – John 3:36; Romans 11:30; Ephesians 2:2
- *merits condemnation by God* – Matthew 12:36; Luke 12:47–48; Matthew 11:20–24
- *leads to death and eternal separation from God* – Romans 6:21–23; 7:13; 2 Thessalonians 1:9

The Bible makes it clear that no man and no woman – with the single exception of Jesus – is as they were made to be; nobody matches God's ideal standard. Different parts of the Scriptures describe this in slightly different ways, but the overall picture is clear.

Humanity has rebelled against God; it has disobeyed God's laws; it has allowed itself to come into a bondage to sin from which it cannot escape by its own efforts. As a result, humanity is blind to its potential and ignorant of God. This is most clearly expressed by the human refusal to believe in Christ – who alone can rescue us from sin, reconcile us with God and restore us to our rightful state.

Responsibility

Genesis 3:1–13 tells the story of the first human sin, and relates how Adam and Eve tried to evade their personal responsibility for their sin: Adam blamed Eve, and Eve blamed the serpent.

Since Eden, people have always tried to blame someone or something for their sin – genes, hormones, upbringing, society, circumstances, and so on. Despite this, every legal system has always been based on the assumption that we are free to choose and responsible for our choices.

Some people argue that we are merely animals at the mercy of our instincts, while others maintain that we are genetically programmed to perform and respond in particular ways.

Nevertheless, every facet of human society has always functioned around the general recognition that men and women are free agents with choice and personal responsibility. All human persuasion (politics, advertising, education, evangelism, etc.), all human praise, and all human blame assume the concept of personal choice and responsibility.

The Bible recognises that there is a tension between the pressures which influence us and our responsibility for our actions and attitudes. It teaches that we have inherited a fallen nature from Adam, and that we are slaves to this sinful nature, the world and its ideas, and demonic forces.

Psalm 103:10–14 ☐
Isaiah 42:1–3 ☐
Matthew 12:15–21 ☐
Luke 23:34 ☐
Acts 3:17 ☐
1 Timothy 1:13 ☐

The Scriptures show that God knows what we are like and that he understands the pressures upon us. As a result, he is patient and gentle with us, he does not treat us as our sins deserve, and he distinguishes between the sins that we commit in ignorance and those that we commit deliberately. We see this in Psalm 103:10–14; Isaiah 42:1–3; Matthew 12:15–21; Luke 23:34; Acts 3:17 and 1 Timothy 1:13.

Deuteronomy 30:15–20 ☐
Joshua 24:15 ☐

But, even though the Bible recognises that our responsibility is reduced by the pressures of sin, God's Word also makes it plain that we remain morally responsible beings. It stresses that we have free choice, it urges us to obey God, and it corrects us when we disobey him. Passages like Deuteronomy 30:15–20 and Joshua 24:15 illustrate our personal responsibility for our choice.

John 5:40 ☐
6:44 ☐

The Bible holds together in creative tension the two parallel truths of God's sovereignty and our human responsibility: Jesus declares them both equally – for example, John 5:40 and 6:44 – and so must we. Whenever we wonder why somebody ignores God's precious message of salvation, we must remember the Scriptures teach that they 'will not' come to Christ and that they 'cannot' come to him. It is both, not either or. We consider this important paradox in Part Eight.

Personal responsibility is a precious gift of God's sovereign grace. It is the gift which makes us uniquely human. In fact, responsibility is the essence of humanity, and is the essential explanation and rationale for the Day of Judgement. Ultimately, if we were not personally responsible for our actions and attitudes, there could be no meaningful judgement.

This shows that, despite our inherited fallen nature, despite the power of Satan, despite the pressure of upbringing and social environment, we are personally responsible for our sinful thoughts and deeds, for our disobedience and presumption, and for all our choices and decisions.

DIVINE HOLINESS

In *Knowing the Father* and *Knowing the Spirit*, we consider the biblical teaching that the triune God is essentially holy. We see this in:

- the Father – Luke 1:49; John 17:11; 1 Peter 1:15–16; Revelation 4:8; 6:10

- the Son – Luke 1:35; Acts 3:14; 4:27–30; 1 John 2:20

- the Spirit – 2 Timothy 1:14; Titus 3:5; 2 Peter 1:21; Jude 20

The word 'holy' has exclusively moral associations for many people: they think that holiness just means being well-behaved. But the Hebrew and Greek words for 'holy', *qadosh* and *hagios*, are functional words which mean 'totally separated to a single purpose' and 'devoted or consecrated to a particular cause'.

The triune God is 'holy' in the sense that he is *totally separated* from all creation by his exalted, eternal, infinite, sinless, morally perfect and spiritual nature: he is 'wholly other', 'wholly beyond'.

This means that the 'holiness' of God is the consequence of the sum of his attributes rather than a particular attribute, and it is this which sets him apart from all creation. We see this, for example, in Exodus 3:5; Leviticus 19:2; Isaiah 6:2–3; 57:15 and 1 John 1:5.

The members of the Trinity, however, are also 'holy' in the sense that they are *totally devoted* to each other. For example, we can say that Jesus reveals his holiness in his consecration to the Father; and that the Spirit reveals his holiness in the way he exists to bring glory only to Jesus. Their absolute commitment to each other is their holiness.

Sin is incompatible with God's full nature, with his holiness, and this effectively separates us from God. The Bible makes it clear that nobody can set eyes upon God's face and survive – even those who

---

Luke 1:49 ☐
John 17:11 ☐
1 Peter 1:15–16 ☐
Revelation 4:8 ☐
6:10 ☐
Luke 1:35 ☐
Acts 3:14 ☐
4:27–30 ☐
1 John 2:20 ☐
2 Timothy 1:14 ☐
Titus 3:5 ☐
2 Peter 1:21 ☐
Jude 20 ☐

Exodus 3:5 ☐
Leviticus 19:2 ☐
Isaiah 6:2–3 ☐
57:15 ☐
1 John 1:5 ☐

glimpse his glory are unable to endure the sight. We see this, for example, in Exodus 3:6; Isaiah 6:1–5; Job 42:5–6; Ezekiel 1:28; Daniel 10:9; Luke 5:8 and Revelation 1:17.

God's holy response to sin is called his 'wrath'. God's wrath is nothing like human anger; instead it is his holy inability to co-exist with sin and his continuous condemnation of sin. By its nature, God's holiness always exposes sin and his wrath always opposes it. Sin cannot approach God, and God cannot tolerate sin.

The Bible uses four metaphors to underline this truth. For example:

- God is often identified as 'high' or 'the Most High'. This name expresses his transcendence and stresses that he is wholly beyond us. We see this in Genesis 14:18–22; Psalm 7:17; 9:2; 21:7; 46:4; 47:2; 57:2; 83:18; 92:8; 93:4; 113:4; Daniel 3:26; 4:2–34; 5:18–21; 7:18–27; Hosea 7:16; 11:7 and Micah 6:6.

- God often warns people not to come too close to him. The arrangements for the Tabernacle and Temple showed that God was among his people, but that they dare not come too close. Sinners cannot approach the holy God with impunity. We see this in Exodus 3:5; 19:3–25; 20:24; 29:45–46; Leviticus 16; Numbers 1:51–53; Joshua 3:4; 1 Samuel 6:19; 2 Samuel 6:6–7; Matthew 7:23 and 25:41.

- God is sometimes described in terms of unapproachable light and all-consuming fire – for example, Deuteronomy 4:24; 1 Timothy 6:16; Hebrews 10:27–31; 12:29 and 1 John 1:5.

- God's rejection of evil is occasionally likened to the human body's rejection of poison by vomiting. God cannot tolerate sin and hypocrisy; they are so utterly repulsive to him that he must expel them from his presence. We see this in Leviticus 18:25–28; 20:22–23; Numbers 21:5; Psalm 95:10; Revelation 3:16.

These metaphors illustrate the complete incompatibility of holiness and sin. As a result of the totality of God's nature, his holiness, God *cannot* be in the presence of sin. If sin approaches God too closely, it is either consumed or repulsed.

Our understanding of God must include the revelation that he hates evil, is disgusted and angered by it, and cannot accept it. And our understanding of salvation must incorporate both the gravity of sin and the brightness of God's glorious holiness.

We will not appreciate our need of the cross if we minimise sin and think of it in terms of rare lapses rather than constant rebellion. And we will be puzzled by the cross if we think that God is an indulgent Father rather than an indignant Creator.

FORGIVENESS

When we finally grasp the seriousness of our sin, and the extent of our personal responsibility, we can begin to appreciate the wonderful grace of forgiveness. But when we understand the awesome magnificence of God's holiness, and the full extent of his wrath against sin, we are bound to start to wonder whether forgiveness can really be possible.

At a superficial level, it may seem natural to enquire why God does not act like the father in the story of the prodigal son appeared to do. But when we think more deeply, we soon realise that forgiveness is by far the hardest act that a holy God could ever perform – much harder than uncomplicated actions like creation and resurrection.

Human sin and divine wrath both stand in the way of our salvation. God must respect us as the responsible beings that he has made in his image; and he must also act consistently with his own nature as a perfectly holy God.

Parts Three to Eight describe how God has dealt with this puzzle and has accomplished our salvation – in Christ, on the cross, by his grace.

Amazingly, the Bible promises that God forgives every aspect of human sin – *hamartia*, Colossians 1:14; *paraptoma*, Colossians 2:13; *parabasis*, Hebrews 9:15; *anomia*, Titus 2:14; and so on. Furthermore, the Scriptures show that God's forgiveness has three distinct aspects:

1. *He remits the punishment due to the presence of sin and removes the barrier which exists between himself and each member of humanity. This is forgiveness of the penalty of sin.*

2. *He removes the offence and erases its memory. He covers the deeds done so that they cannot be seen or remembered by him again. This is forgiveness from the guilt of sin.*

Colossians 1:14 ☐
2:13 ☐
Hebrews 9:15 ☐
Titus 2:14 ☐

3. *He destroys the life of the sin force in a spiritual operation which removes the moral compulsion to do wrong. This is forgiveness from the power of sin.*

Romans 6:1–23 ☐

Colossians 1:13–14 ☐

Romans 6 describes this aspect of forgiveness as 'death to sin' and Colossians 1:13–14 calls it 'our freedom'.

Human forgiveness

In everyday life, human forgiveness is an active process which goes on inside the mind of someone who has been hurt or wronged. When we forgive someone, we knock down the barrier between us and the culprit so that we are free to relate amicably again.

True human forgiveness is much more than not taking revenge against someone who has hurt us, more than merely ignoring a hurt, and more than just not punishing a person for their wrong.

Real forgiveness involves a change which starts in our thoughts, then expresses itself in our actions, and finally reshapes our feelings. We sweep the fault away from our thoughts, and end its negative influence on our actions and emotions. We may still be aware of the fault, but it not longer counts as something which matters to us.

Before forgiveness, the fault provoked a barrier of resentment, anger, mistrust, dislike, and so on. After forgiveness has been given *and* received, those who were estranged can move on to live in peace.

Divine forgiveness

Human forgiveness is not a miniature replica of God's forgiveness. The Bible shows God forgiving men and women with such a depth, and to such an extent, that even the best example of human forgiveness is only a faint echo or feeble imitation of God's forgiveness.

The Bible complements this, however, by also describing the way that God moves against sin with all the passion of his wrath.

Somehow, we must resist the temptation to focus on only one of these truths – forgiveness and justice exist together, and both lose their meaning when separated. Most human parents soon learn that love and fairness must exist alongside each other if they are to care for their children properly!

Whenever the holy God encounters evil, he must respond against it: for love must confront evil with purity if it is to remain love. God would not be more loving if did not punish sin in the act of forgiving it, he would not be God and he would not be loving.

Yet, despite the sin against which God's indignation blazes, the Father takes the amazing step of grace and receives sinful people as his intimate friends. This can seem too easy, too good to be true – especially when we realise how strongly the holy God condemns our lusts and selfish thoughts. But this mixture of forgiveness and condemnation is the heart of salvation – and is always seen in Jesus. It is in him that divine forgiveness personally appears and approaches.

Divine forgiveness is an inexplicable gift of pure love to unworthy sinners which contains the solution to humanity's deepest problems. As we see in *Knowing the Father*, God takes the initiative. 'Our Father, Our Redeemer' makes the first move. The Judge of all humanity brings guilty sinners into the enjoyment of the Father's love – provided that they choose to be brought in and respond willingly to his love.

The Father's grace

Many believers hear more about the price of forgiveness and the cost of salvation than about the free-and-overflowing grace of the Father who, in his passionate desire for the homecoming of sinners, gave up his only Son.

We do not need to understand everything about salvation to receive it. We are not required to appreciate the full cost of forgiveness before we can benefit from it – we can learn about this later.

In fact, the only condition of forgiveness is that we respond to the Father's grace with humble, outstretched arms and a thankful, joyful heart. We simply come to the Father, like the lost son in the parable, and take God at his word.

If we do not look to the Father and his grace, if he is not the focus of our faith and salvation, we may present a message which suggests that the best people can hope is that God can be persuaded into some sort of uncomfortable tolerance of sinners by Jesus.

We may think that returning sons and daughters still need to keep their distance from the Father, and that our gratitude should be showered upon Jesus for somehow twisting the Father's arm to allow us into a back-room of the family home as the lowest form of servant.

This sort of unbiblical thinking leads to passivity, fear, self-condemnation, low expectations, a lack of boldness, and legalism.

This may have been how the prodigal son felt while he was trudging home, but it does not represent the father in Jesus' parable, and it is a terrible caricature of the heavenly Father who sent his Son into a far country to make a way home, and who is now waiting with longing to usher us into his presence as sons and daughters with unconditional grace and uninhibited celebration.

To be a believer is to know that the Father has defined our identity through the cross and that he now calls us his sons and daughters. He beckons us to come forward and receive the inheritance of our salvation – the robe of sonship, the ring of authority, the sandals of freedom, and so on.

It is this free grace of the Father which initiates the sending of the Son and sets up salvation – so that the Father may open his arms and welcome the multitudes of children who are brought to glory by the Son through the Spirit.

PART TWO

self-consistency

When people ask why Jesus' death on the cross was really necessary for salvation, Christians have traditionally used the language of 'satisfaction' in their answers.

Although the words 'satisfy' and 'satisfaction' do not appear in the Bible in relation to the cross, church leaders in every century and tradition have always maintained that some sort of 'satisfaction' was necessary before the holy God could forgive sin. But they have always disagreed about *what* or *who* was satisfied – and *why*.

Satan satisfied

Right from the time of the Greek Church in the second century, some leaders have insisted that the death of Christ on the cross was the price which Satan demanded for the release of his captives, and that Christ endured the cross to satisfy the devil's rights.

However, just as some believers ignore Satan or under-estimate his power, so this idea over-estimates his power and authority. Although the devil did hold humanity captive from Eden to the cross, and he was lord of sin and death, and Jesus did come to liberate us from him, Satan has always been only a rebel and a usurper. He may have gained some 'rights' over humanity through sin, but he has never acquired any rights which God has 'needed' to 'satisfy'.

In Part Seven, we consider the full extent of the devil's defeat at Calvary. While we must remember that Jesus has triumphed decisively, and has delivered us from Satan's bondage, we should not think that Satan had a right which God was obliged to satisfy.

The Law satisfied

Since Ambrose (a fourth century Latin 'Father'), there have always been Christians who explain the cross by insisting that the Law needed to be satisfied. They argue that sin disregards and disobeys God's Law, and that sinners incur an automatic penalty by breaking the Law.

They insist that the Law had to be upheld and its penalties paid – sinners could not simply be 'let off'. The cross, therefore, was necessary to satisfy the requirements of the Law.

Daniel 6:1–17 ☐

These believers often use Daniel 6 to support their argument. Although King Darius respected Daniel and wanted to save him, the Persian law had to take its course – the penalty had to be paid. In the same way, they argue, God loves sinners and longs to save us, but he cannot violate the Law which has condemned us – hence the cross.

But God is not caught like Darius in some technical muddle, whereby he is almost tricked into the cross; and the Law is not an inflexible legal code with automatic penalties which determine God's actions.

Galatians 3:10–13 ☐

There is some truth in this emphasis on the Law, for Galatians 3:10–13 plainly teaches that Christ redeemed us from the curse of the Law by becoming a curse for us. But this is not the same as teaching that the Law itself needed to be satisfied.

Just as our deliverance from Satan does not mean that he had rights which God had to satisfy, so our release from the Law does not mean that it had demands which God had to satisfy. Redemption and victory are consequences of the cross, not its essential causes.

In *Knowing the Son*, we see that submission was at the heart of Jesus' sonship. At one level, we can say that Jesus' submission to the Law was indispensable to our rescue from its condemnation – for he both fulfilled the demands of the Law and endured its condemnation. The deeper truth, however, is that Jesus submitted to the person of the Father rather than to the principles of the Law; and that his submission to the Law in fulfilment and endurance was merely a consequence of his personal submission to the Father.

Just as God owed Satan no duty, so he was not held prisoner by the Law. The truth is that God was the Creator of the Law, and the Law condemns sin only because it has its source in the holy God.

In *Living Faith* and *Listening to God*, we see that every Word from God is a self-revelation of God. This means that the holy Law reveals the holy God: the demands of the Law – including its condemnation and curse of sin – cannot be separated from the nature of God himself.

This suggests that it is probably far more accurate to think in terms of the holy God needing personally to be satisfied, than it is to stress that an independent, impersonal set of rules somehow had to be satisfied.

God's honour and justice satisfied

Today, most evangelicals believe that God owed nothing to the devil except punishment for his rebellion, but that humanity owed something to God. They identify this as the debt which needed to be paid, to be satisfied, on the cross. We consider this in Part Five.

Some leaders portray God as the Victim of sin and explain the cross in terms of satisfying God's 'honour' – an idea which began with Anselm, an eleventh century Archbishop of Canterbury.

Others present God as the Judge of sin and explain the cross in terms of satisfying his 'justice'. This idea began in the thirteenth century with Thomas Aquinas and Duns Scotus, was developed after the Reformation by Calvin and Cranmer, and was incorporated into the Westminster Confession in 1647.

Leaders who stress God's 'honour' argue that, by our sin (by not acknowledging God as Lord, and not submitting fully to him) we have stolen the honour due to God. And, because of his holiness, God cannot ignore this theft. They reason that, if we are to be forgiven, we must repay the stolen honour. But we cannot. Our present obedience cannot make up for our past sins, because this is required of us anyway, and no other sinner can make satisfaction for us.

They say that, in his grace, God sent Jesus as a 'fully-God, fully-human' being to offer his sinless life to satisfy the offended honour of God, and they conclude that Jesus' gracious offering of his absolute perfection repaid the honour which humanity had stolen.

Those who focus on God as Judge, and stress the satisfaction of his justice, maintain that there is a fundamental and irreconcilable disagreement between God's righteousness and our unrighteousness.

They insist that God's constant holy wrath against the sin of the whole world needs to be placated, exhausted, satisfied; and that the Father sent the 'fully-God, fully-human' sinless Son to satisfy the demands of God's justice against sin and make forgiveness possible.

Of course, most Christians do not stick rigidly to one idea about satisfaction. For example, many teach that the demands of God's Law were satisfied by Christ's perfect obedience in his life and death, and that God's justice was also satisfied by his perfect sacrifice for sin which bore the Law's penalty in his death.

GOD HIMSELF

The truth, however, is that – on their own – each one of these ideas is an inadequate explanation of satisfaction. It is surely not the Law, or divine honour or holy justice which needs to be satisfied, but God himself. He is not just the Victim of sin, or only the Law-Maker, or simply the Judge – he is all of them, and more.

The problem with speaking about satisfying Law, honour, justice, and so on, is we can suggest that God is controlled by something which is exterior to him. It is God himself, in the total fullness (the absolute holiness) of his personal being, who needs to be satisfied – not a particular aspect of God or a code or quality which is outside of him.

Self-consistency

Some people react against the idea of divine self-satisfaction because of its unpleasant human counterpart. They think that those who try to satisfy themselves lack self-control, and that those who express self-satisfaction lack humility.

God, however, is perfect: he has absolute self-control and infinite humility. This means that divine self-satisfaction is entirely different from human self-satisfaction.

When we say that God must satisfy himself we mean that he must be himself, that he must be true to his nature, that he must act consistently with the perfection of his nature.

The Scriptures stress that God cannot disown himself, cannot contradict himself, cannot lie. He is never arbitrary, unpredictable or capricious. He is always true to himself, always consistent with his nature, always 'all-himself'. We see this, for example, in Deuteronomy 32:4; Psalm 89:33; 2 Timothy 2:13; Titus 1:2 and Hebrews 6:18.

Deuteronomy 32:4 ☐
Psalm 89:33 ☐
2 Timothy 2:13 ☐
Titus 1:2 ☐
Hebrews 6:18 ☐

The Bible underlines God's self-satisfaction, his self-consistency, in four main ways. These show that God judges sinners simply because he must – he must remain true to himself and be perfectly 'self-consistent'.

1. The provocation of God

In the Old Testament, God describes himself as being 'provoked' to anger and jealousy by Israel's idolatry, and the prophets frequently repeat this idea.

We see this, for example, in Deuteronomy 32:16–21; Judges 2:12; 1 Kings 15:30; 21:22; 2 Kings 17:17; 22:17; Psalm 78:58; Jeremiah 32:30–32; Ezekiel 8:17 and Hosea 12:14.

Deuteronomy 32:16–21 ☐
Judges 2:12 ☐
1 Kings 15:30 ☐
21:22 ☐
2 Kings 17:17 ☐
22:17 ☐
Psalm 78:58 ☐
Jeremiah 32:30–32 ☐
Ezekiel 8:17 ☐
Hosea 12:14 ☐

This does not mean that God was irritated by Israel's behaviour. The biblical language of provocation merely expresses God's *inevitable* response to evil. Within God, there is a holy intolerance of sin – especially idolatry. Whenever and wherever sin occurs, it always 'provokes' God's wrath.

God is never provoked without a good reason. Only sin provokes him – and it must provoke him if God is to be and behave like God. Quite simply, if God was not provoked by the opposite of his nature he would not be God.

2. God's burning wrath

The Scriptures often describe God's anger in terms of 'burning', 'kindling', 'consuming', 'raging', and so on. Passages like Joshua 7:1; 23:16; Judges 3:8; 2 Samuel 24:1; 2 Kings 13:3; 22:13 and Hosea 8:5 describe how God burns with anger when he sees his people disobeying his Law and breaking his covenant.

The Old Testament shows that God 'burns' with anger when he is 'provoked' or 'aroused' by sin. We see this, for example, in Deuteronomy 29:27–28; 2 Kings 22:17; Psalm 79:5; Jeremiah 4:4; 21:12; Ezekiel 36:5–6; 38:19; Zephaniah 1:18 and 3:8.

The fire of anger is God's inevitable response to evil – yet it never rages out of control. Exodus 32:10; Jeremiah 44:22 and Ezekiel 24:13–14. show that God *cannot* endure rebellion; and Psalm 78:38; Isaiah 48:9; Lamentations 3:22; Romans 2:4 and 2 Peter 3:9 describe how he mercifully restrains his anger.

However, once the fire of God's anger is 'kindled' it is extremely hard to put out. We see this, for example, in 2 Kings 23:26; 22:17; 2 Chronicles 34:25 and Jeremiah 21:12. When God's anger burns against people, it consumes them – as in Numbers 11:1; Deuteronomy 4:24; 6:15; Psalm 59:13; Isaiah 10:17; 30:27; Lamentations 2:3; Ezekiel 22:31 and Zephaniah 1:18. And his anger subsides only when judgement is complete or a radical change has occurred. We see this in Joshua 7:26; Jeremiah 4:4; 21:12; Ezekiel 5:13; 16:42 and 21:17.

This establishes that there is something in God's holiness which is provoked, aroused and ignited by evil – we call this 'his wrath': this then burns until the evil is consumed and the wrath is 'satisfied'.

3. God's complete satisfaction

The Hebrew word *kalah* is often used in the Old Testament in association with God's anger. *Kalah* means the end of something and is variously translated as 'to complete', 'to end', 'to finish', 'to consume', 'to accomplish', 'to exhaust' and 'to satisfy'.

Kalah is often used in the Old Testament to show that time, work and life all come to an end, that tears are completed by weeping, that grass is finished in drought, that human strength is exhausted by exercise, and so on.

Joshua 7:1 ☐
23:16 ☐
Judges 3:8 ☐
2 Samuel 24:1 ☐
2 Kings 13:3 ☐
22:13 ☐
Hosea 8:5 ☐
Deuteronomy
29:27–28 ☐
2 Kings 22:17 ☐
Psalm 79:5 ☐
Jeremiah 4:4 ☐
21:12 ☐
Ezekiel 36:5–6 ☐
38:19 ☐
Zephaniah 1:18 ☐
3:8 ☐
Psalm 78:38 ☐
Isaiah 48:9 ☐
Lamentations
3:22 ☐
Romans 2:4 ☐
2 Peter 3:9 ☐
Exodus 32:10 ☐
Jeremiah 44:22 ☐
Ezekiel 24:13–14 ☐
2 Kings 23:26 ☐
22:17 ☐
2 Chronicles
34:25 ☐
Jeremiah 21:12 ☐
Numbers 11:1 ☐
Deuteronomy
4:24 ☐
6:15 ☐
Psalm 59:13 ☐
Isaiah 10:17 ☐
30:27 ☐
Lamentations 2:3 ☐
Ezekiel 22:31 ☐
Zephaniah 1:18 ☐
Joshua 7:26 ☐
Jeremiah 4:4 ☐
21:12 ☐
Ezekiel 5:13 ☐
16:42 ☐
21:17 ☐

SELF-CONSISTENCY

Kalah is used by the prophets, however, to show that God will 'exhaust', 'satisfy', 'complete' his anger upon his people. We see this, for example, in Ezekiel 5:13; 6:12; 7:7–8; 13:15; 20:8, 21 and Lamentations 4:11.

Kalah suggests that God's anger ceases only when it has been fully satisfied. This is not because God is a tyrant; it is because whatever exists within him must be expressed, and what is expressed must be completed or finished.

When we take these three pictures together, we see that God is 'provoked' to jealous anger by sin; that, once his wrath is kindled, it 'burns' until it is 'satisfied' or 'completed' and the sin is fully 'consumed'; and that this wrath flows inevitably from God's character and is a manifestation or revelation of his holiness.

4. God's Name

The fourth way the Bible emphasises God's self-consistency is by using God's name. We consider the Name of God in *Knowing the Father*, and see that 'the Name' stands for God himself, and refers to the total revelation of all that is known about him. For example:

- *'the name of the Lord' was proclaimed to Moses when God passed before him and announced his nature* – Exodus 34:5–6

- *to 'call upon the name of the Lord' was to worship him as God* – Genesis 21:33; 26:25

- *to 'forget his name' was to depart from God* – Jeremiah 23:27

- *to 'take the name of the Lord in vain' was to affront his divine majesty* – Exodus 20:7

We can say that the biblical phrase 'the Name of God' encapsulates the full glorious nature and character of God. It points to the total manifestation of God to his people.

In the Old Testament, God's Name was the pledge of all that he had promised to be to Israel and to do for them. We see this, for example, in 1 Samuel 12:22 and Psalm 25:11.

For Israel, the phrase, 'the Name of the Lord', enshrined the most important facts of their revelation and experience of God. The all-powerful Maker of heaven and earth was their God. He had called them into a covenant relationship of grace. The conviction that God will never deny his covenant, or go back on his promises, or be anything other than fully 'self-consistent', lies behind almost every use of the phrase, 'the Name of the Lord'.

The Old Testament makes it clear that God always acts according to his Name, in a manner which is consistent with the totality of his nature – with his holiness. We see this, for example, in Jeremiah 14:1–21; Ezekiel 20:44 and 36:1–23.

Jeremiah 14:1–21 ☐
Ezekiel 20:44 ☐
36:1–23 ☐

When God acts for the sake of his Name he is not protecting himself from misrepresentation, he is merely being self-consistent. God is concerned for his reputation, but he is compelled by his character to be continually consistent – to satisfy himself.

This means that God is God. He cannot deny any part of his nature – he cannot be inconsistent or contradict himself – because he is always true to all of himself. He never deviates from being fully who he is. As we see in *Knowing the Father*, this is expressed by God's personal name, *Yahweh*, which means 'I am who I am'. God is who he is; he is his holy self; he cannot be anything else.

GOD'S JUST LOVE

God's self-consistency means he must forgive sinners and reconcile them to himself in a way which is fully consistent with his character.

For salvation to be effective, God must conquer the devil to capture his captives; he must satisfy his Law, his justice, his honour and his wrath. But even more importantly, he must satisfy himself – God must satisfy every aspect of his infinite being, including his justice *and* love.

Hosea 11:1–11 ☐

Hosea 11:1–11 hints at the redemptive tension which God experiences when his justice and love appear to conflict. Israel, God's child, deserved to be punished for its spiritual adultery and wilful refusal to repent, but how could God destroy his own child?

This is the creative tension between what God should do because of his justice and what he cannot do because of his love, the eternal tension within God between his compassion and his wrath.

Parallel and inter-related attributes

Throughout the Scriptures, in both Testaments, in the words of Jesus and of Paul, God's love and God's wrath are held together in perfect tension to show that we must not think about one aspect of his nature without remembering its counterpart. For example:

- *he is merciful and gracious, but he does not leave the guilty unpunished* – Exodus 34:6–7
- *mercy and truth meet together in him, and righteousness and peace kiss each other* – Psalm 85:10
- *he is a just God and a Saviour* – Isaiah 45:21
- *there is mercy in his wrath* – Micah 7:18; Habakkuk 3:2
- *he is full of grace and truth* – John 1:14
- *he is just and the justifier* – Romans 3:26
- *he is good and severe* – Romans 11:22
- *he is full of wrath and rich in mercy* – Ephesians 2:3–4
- *he is faithful and just* – 1 John 1:9

It is sloppy to think that, for example, God is simply love. This is true, but it is not the full truth, for no one human word can fully describe God's infinite nature.

We have noted that the Bible uses the phrase 'the Name' to point to the totality of God's nature, and that God's 'holiness' or 'total separation' is the consequence of the sum of his attributes. There is danger in concentrating on one aspect of God's character because he is filled with attributes which seem to be opposites but which are – in reality – perfectly balanced and closely inter-related.

The Bible handles this by presenting, for example, God's love and wrath, his goodness and righteousness, his mercy and justice, his transcendence and immanence, and so on, as parallel, inter-related truths which can be seen on earth in opposition but which unite in the glorious infinity of God himself.

We must not try to mix these paradoxical attributes together into one theological concoction, because this destroys the biblical revelation of the mystery of God – which always stresses the continuous, simultaneous revelation of all the parallel aspects of God's nature.

In Part Six, we consider God's work of revelation on the cross, and see how God manifests his wrath and his love in one event. The cross is the supreme revelation of God's infinite love *and* his all-consuming anger, his inflexible righteousness *and* his gracious mercy, and so on.

The cross shows that these attributes are not irreconcilable, and are not in turmoil. In fact they magnify each other, for we grasp the greatness of God's love in the cross only when we appreciate the full extent of his anger on the cross.

God is not at odds with himself. There is no contradiction within him, for there can be no conflict within God. He is never uncertain about his actions or confused in his plans. He exists in eternal equilibrium. He is the God of perfect peace, but it is a peace which holds his related attributes in a perfect creative tension.

If we are to understand salvation at all accurately, we must have a biblical picture of God – which is why *Knowing the Father* comes before this book in the *Sword of the Spirit* series.

God is not an indulgent 'daddy' who compromises his holiness to spare and spoil us; and he is not a vindictive 'tyrant' who suppresses his love to crush and destroy us. Instead, the Creator of heaven and earth is both fatherly and sovereign. The king of the universe never acts tyrannically because he is a Father; and the righteous judge always acts mercifully because he is shaped by his loving fatherhood.

The whole of our Christian faith hangs on our knowledge of God; and the whole purpose of salvation is that we might know the Father – accurately, intimately, personally and eternally.

So how can God 'satisfy' his justice and wrath without consuming us? How can he 'satisfy' his love without condoning our sins? How can he simultaneously save us and satisfy himself? How can he be fully 'self-consistent'?

These are the hard questions which are at the heart of the cross – the place where God substituted and sacrificed himself for the salvation of all humanity.

PART THREE

substitution and sacrifice

God's self-satisfaction, his self-consistency, means that he is always true to the whole of himself. He does not act in one set of circumstances according to one attribute, and then – in a different set of circumstances – act according to another. God never manifests one attribute at the expense of another – for they are all connected and all inter-related. He always expresses the fullness of his character.

We have seen that the hardest question associated with forgiveness is, 'How can God can be true to all of himself?' How can he simultaneously express both his holy wrath in condemnation and judgement *and* also his merciful love in compassion and pardon?

From the earliest days of the church, the Christian answer has always been that God satisfied himself (that he acted self-consistently) by providing a 'substitute' for the sinner. In this way, the substitute endures the condemnation and judgement while the sinner enjoys the compassion and pardon.

In his infinite mercy, God willed to forgive us, and, in his eternal righteousness, he willed to forgive us righteously – without ignoring and condoning our sin. God acted self-consistently by focusing the fullness of his just wrath on the substitute whom he graciously provided (himself in the person of his very own Son) and by pouring the fullness of his merciful love onto us – undeserving sinners.

We have seen that, throughout the ages, different church traditions have wrestled with the Bible to understand *who* and *what* was satisfied on the cross. They have also wrestled with God's 'self-substitution' and the nature of the substitute – for the Bible does not reveal these simply and clearly. If we are to understand substitution at all biblically, we need to consider the Old Testament sacrifices – which prepare the way for the substitutionary sacrifice of God-in-Christ on the cross.

OLD TESTAMENT SACRIFICES

It is impossible to read the New Testament without realising that the writers recognised Christ's death as a sacrifice. We see this, for example, in Matthew 20:28; John 3:16; 10:17–18; Romans 3:25; 4:25; 8:3, 32; 1 Corinthians 5:7–8; 2 Corinthians 5:18–21; Galatians 1:4; 2:20; Ephesians 5:2, 25; 1 Timothy 2:6; Titus 2:14; Hebrews 9:14, 26; 1 Peter 3:18 and 1 John 4:9–10.

The Old Testament sacrificial system is behind the New Testament thinking about Christ's death. This is seen most clearly in Hebrews, which stresses that the sacrifice of Jesus is the ultimate reality towards which all the 'foreshadows' of the Old Testament system point.

The first sacrifice

The Bible teaches that sacrifice began with God. He made the first sacrifice. He spilt the first blood. He endured the first grief of loss. His example in Genesis 3:21 established the pattern and principles for all future sacrifices, and paved the way for the cross.

God graciously offered the condemned humans skin tunics to cover their sin and clothe them for their new task outside Eden. It is implicit that some animals must have died to provide those tunics of grace. And it must have been God himself who slew, then skinned, the precious, perfect animals that he had only just made and blessed.

This incident sets the tone for the rest of the Old Testament teaching about sacrifices, and clearly points to God's final-and-ultimate sacrifice. We see, for example, that:

- *those who benefited were completely undeserving*
- *those who suffered were totally blameless*
- *the sacrifice was permanent*
- *blood was shed*
- *the sacrifice was in a perfect condition – only the best would do*
- *the cost was considerable for both the 'sacrificer' and the sacrifice, the giver and the gift*
- *grace, love and mercy were the motivating emotions*
- *the beneficiaries were free to accept or reject the proffered gift*
- *the sacrifice must have been puzzling, for there were many more fig-leaves in the vicinity – even if they were useless on frosty days*

The first human sacrifices

Genesis 4:3–5 describes the first sacrifices offered by humans to God. Cain and Abel presented gifts to God; and Luke 11:50–51 and Hebrews 11:4 seem to explain why God looked favourably on Abel's sacrifice. Abel was a prophet, and he sacrificed the first-born of his flock.

Genesis 4:3–5 ☐

Hebrews 11:4 ☐

Nothing in the context suggests that these first human sacrifices were made only to earn God's favour or to placate him; there seems to be a real element of thanksgiving.

Noah made the next sacrifice. Genesis 8:20 shows that, after the Flood had subsided, Noah built an altar and offered God a burnt-offering of birds and beasts in thanks for his family's deliverance. This was the fourth example of Noah's obedience – Genesis 6:22; 7:5; 8:15–18, 20 – and God was so pleased with Noah's obedient sacrifice that he rewarded him, in 8:21–9:17, with the promise of glorious blessing.

Genesis 8:20 ☐

Genesis 6:22 ☐
7:5 ☐
8:15–18 ☐
8:21–9:17 ☐
22:7 ☐

Abraham must have been in the habit of offering God sacrifices from his flocks or Isaac would not have asked about the lamb in Genesis 22:7. In this chapter, God asked for the first time for a sacrifice – and he wanted the best.

Abraham was ordered to offer Isaac as a burnt-offering on Mount Moriah – the place where the Jerusalem Temple would eventually be sited. Isaac, who by then seems to have been aged about thirty (he was thirty seven when Sarah died a few verses later) was prepared to be the willing victim; and his elderly father was ready to sacrifice his only son. But how puzzling the death must have seemed to them both, especially after all God's promises through the years.

Faith and sacrifice were first linked with reference to Abel; and, by faith, Abraham seized the knife and prepared to plunge it into his son. As we have seen, human reasoning always concludes that sacrifice is unnecessary – but Abraham believed that God knew best.

Genesis 22:14 ☐

Abraham did not understand why God wanted him to sacrifice his son. Even though he uttered a remarkable prophecy in 22:14, he did not know that, nearly 2,000 years later, God would go through similar but stronger agonies on the same mountain. Abraham simply acted with faith and prepared to obey God.

Genesis 22:15–18 ☐

Genesis 22:15–18 describes how God responded to Abraham's willingness to sacrifice his son with a sworn promise of great blessing. Abraham and Isaac had been ready for death without a reward – loving obedience was their only motivation. But God's grace intervened, provided a substitute victim, then rewarded the sacrifice with blessing: this link between sacrifice and blessing is repeated in Genesis 46:1–4.

Genesis 46:1–4 ☐

The Passover

The Egyptians endured ten plagues because Pharaoh would not allow the Israelites to visit the wilderness to worship God with sacrifices. Exodus 10:24–26 reveals two principles of Old Testament sacrifice.

Exodus 10:24–26 ☐

First, people had to allow God to direct their sacrifices; and, second, they could offer only clean animals and birds which actually belonged to them – there had to be genuine costly self-denial.

The tenth plague was a supreme act of holy judgement on Egypt *and* a merciful act of deliverance for Israel. The Passover, in Exodus 11–13, was the simultaneous evidence of both God's love *and* his justice, his grace *and* his holiness.

Exodus 11–13 ☐

As with Adam and Eve in Eden, each family had personally to appropriate God's provision: the sacrifice of their best animal, and

SUBSTITUTION AND SACRIFICE

the sprinkling of its blood on their door-posts, was their faith-filled response to God's grace. And, once again, God rewarded his people's obedient sacrifices with blessing – this time a personal deliverance from death and a national deliverance from slavery.

Exodus 12:2 shows that the original Passover sacrifice was the beginning of Israel's corporate, national life; so the New Testament identifies Christ's death as taking place at the Passover, as the fulfilment of the Passover, and as the beginning of the new redeemed community. We see this, for example, in John 1:29, 36; 13:1; 18:28; 19:14; 1 Corinthians 5:7–8 and Revelation 5:6, 9, 12; 12:11.

Through the Passover, God simultaneously revealed himself as:

- *Judge* – God's holy wrath 'passed through' Egypt and condemned every firstborn male. There was no discrimination between creatures or classes of people. There was only one way of escape, and that was by God's gracious provision.

- *Redeemer* – God's merciful love 'passed over' every blood-marked home to shield them from his wrath.

- *Covenant maker-and-keeper* – God redeemed the Israelites to make them his people. They belonged to God because they had been purchased by the blood and so were consecrated to his service. We consider this more fully in Parts Four and Eight.

It should be obvious that these 'foreshadowing' truths were fully revealed at Calvary. It is important we recognise that the Judge and the Redeemer are the same divine person. The God who *passed through* Egypt was the same God who *passed over* the blood-sprinkled homes.

We stress in *Knowing the Father* that we should not characterise the Father as the Judge and the Son as the Redeemer. It is the one God who, through Christ, condemns sin and saves humanity.

The Passover also teaches that:

- *salvation is by substitution* – the only first-born males who were spared were those in homes where a first-born lamb had died instead of them

- *salvation is through a faith-filled appropriation* – after it had been shed, the blood had to be appropriated by being sprinkled over the door-posts

---

John 1:29, 36 ☐
13:1 ☐
18:28 ☐
19:14 ☐

1 Corinthians
5:7–8 ☐

Revelation
5:6–12 ☐
12:11 ☐

Ritual sacrifices

After the Passover, while Israel was wandering in the wilderness, God gave Moses clear instructions about sacrifice. We can read brief outlines in Exodus 20:24–26; 22:29–30; 23:14–19; 29; Leviticus 17; 23; Numbers 15; Deuteronomy 12 and 16. The fullest description is found in Leviticus 1–7, and this sets out the five principal rituals:

- *the holocaust, or burnt offering*
- *the oblation, or grain offering*
- *the communion, or peace offering*
- *the sin offering*
- *the guilt, reparation or trespass offering*

We can say that:

- the *oblation* and *communion* sacrifices helped the people to express their feelings of being creatures who belonged to God;
- the *holocaust* sacrifice represented the people's dedication – and God's acceptance – of everything that they had and were;
- the eating together by priest and people in the *communion* sacrifice reminded them of their vital relationship with God;
- the *sin* and *guilt* sacrifices enabled the people both to display their human sense of separation from a holy God caused by their sin and guilt, and to cry to God for him to cover it.

Despite these distinctions, all the sacrifices stressed God's gracious initiative and the people's absolute dependence on him and his grace.

In all the sacrifices, only the best would do. We have seen that the worshippers had to sacrifice in a way which depleted their personal resources, but Deuteronomy 23:18 suggests that even this would be unacceptable if the property had been unlawfully acquired.

Male animals were preferred to females, and the mature first-born was considered the best-of-all. They had to be perfect specimens: the creature chosen for sacrifice was always the one which would have most improved its owner's flocks.

God's justice meant that the poor were not penalised by these demands. Leviticus 5:7–13 shows that those who were unable to afford a sheep or a goat could offer two doves instead. And, if they could not manage even this, an offering of grain would suffice.

The ritual sacrifices were meant to be offered personally and nationally, privately and publicly, regularly and as special needs arose. Numbers 28–29 list the daily, weekly, monthly and annual public sacrifices; and Exodus 12 shows how the Passover was to be celebrated within the family.

Whenever the Israelites turned to God, they were supposed to worship him by offering him sacrifices. The Bible shows that the ritual sacrifices were offered:

- *to fulfil a vow* – 2 Samuel 15:7–9
- *to release a person from a vow* – Numbers 6
- *as a spontaneous act of worship* – Judges 13:17–23
- *to purify a leper after healing and a woman after childbirth* – Leviticus 12; 14
- *at the ordination of a priest and the offering of a levite to God* – Leviticus 8; Numbers 8
- *at times of national repentance* – 1 Samuel 7
- *when battle was near* – 1 Samuel 13:8–12
- *at royal coronations* – 1 Kings 1:9
- *at the dedication of sanctuaries* – 1 Kings 8:1–13

The Old Testament ritual sacrifices had six stages, and each one was as significant as the other five.

1. *The worshippers selected or purchased their sacrifices and brought them to the designated place.*

2. *If the offering was an animal, they placed their hands on it to show that it was their representative or substitute. If they were making a sin or guilt offering, they confessed their sins symbolically to transfer the legal consequences to the animal.*

3. *The worshipper personally killed the animal.*

4. *The priests collected the blood in a basin and poured it against two opposite corners of the altar so that all four sides were sprinkled with the blood.*

Numbers 28–29 ☐
Exodus 12 ☐

2 Samuel 15:7–9 ☐
Numbers 6 ☐
Judges 13:17–23 ☐
Leviticus 12 ☐
14 ☐
8 ☐
Numbers 8 ☐
1 Samuel 7 ☐
13:8–12 ☐
1 Kings 1:9 ☐
8:1–13 ☐

5. *The fat was burnt. If it was a holocaust offering, everything was burnt except the skin.*

6. *What remained of the sacrifice was eaten by the priests. If it was a communion sacrifice, the remainder was eaten by priests and worshippers together.*

The holocaust and communion sacrifices were used for celebration and thanksgiving, the consecration of persons and objects for holy service, and for the removal of ceremonial uncleanness.

The other sacrifices, however, had a far deeper purpose. Leviticus repeatedly states that a person's sin and reparation offerings 'would be accepted as effectual for their atonement'. The Hebrew word *kaphar* is usually translated as 'to atone', but it really means 'to cover'. This means that the sin and reparation sacrifices covered the worshippers' sins and made restitution for their guilt.

Just as the first sacrifice was offered by God's blood-stained hands as cover for Adam's sin and clothing for his new task, so – through the ritual sacrifices – God provided his people with a series of sacrifices which could go on covering their sin and enabling them to serve him.

The Servant songs

As time went by, the ritualistic system of sacrifice was abused, and the realisation grew that the system was not final. God's prophets began to plead for an extra type of sacrifice, for practical actions as well as, not instead of, symbolic gestures, for personal morality to be wedded to legal ritual.

This critical development in the prophetic awareness of God's desires is seen in, for example, Psalm 50:8–23; 51:16–19; Proverbs 15:8; 21:27; Isaiah 1:11–20; 58:1–14; 66:1–4, 18–21; Jeremiah 6:20; 7:21–28; Hosea 8:11–13; Amos 5:21–24 and Micah 6:6–8.

This understanding of sacrifice as both a ceremony for personal 'atonement' and also a continuous holy way of life reached its Old Testament climax in the four songs of the servant of the Lord recorded in Isaiah 42:1–9; 49:1–6; 50:4–11 and 52:13–53:12. These songs present a person whose death makes sacrificial, substitutionary atonement for others *and* whose life is characterised by love, justice, humility, suffering and self-sacrifice.

The first three songs reveal that this mysterious servant is an individual formed by God and called by him while still in his mother's womb. He is a disciple who is filled with God's Spirit. He establishes justice on earth so that he may instruct humanity and judge us by his Word. He works gently, quietly and discreetly. He appears to fail, accepts outrage and contempt, but does not give up because *Yahweh* himself sustains him.

The fourth song describes the appalling sufferings of the servant who, though innocent, is treated as a sinner punished by God and condemned to die a shameful death. It shows that all this is the servant's voluntary offering for sinners whose sin and guilt he takes onto himself and for whom he intercedes. And the song reveals that, by a previously unimaginable act of power, God accepts the atoning sacrifice of his servant and brings about the salvation of all humanity.

These extraordinary prophetic songs point to Jesus. In fact, all the Old Testament sacrifices point in some way to him, for they express a need which only he fully satisfies, and embody a faith which he alone can justify. But, more than that, they demand a lifestyle which only he makes possible. The victim slain may have been a substitute, but the worshippers always had to deny themselves in some way for God.

These two principles are central to salvation by grace. Christ may have died in our place permanently to cover our sin, unite us with each other and bring us to God; but self-denial is still the ritual demanded of the lives that he rules.

SIN-BEARING

New Testament passages like 1 Peter 2:24 and Hebrews 9:28 teach that Jesus 'bore our sins' on the cross. Through the centuries, in every tradition of the church, Christians have traditionally understood this to mean that Jesus was the innocent God-provided substitute who took the place of guilty humanity and endured the penalty due to its sin.

During the twentieth century, however, many teachers have challenged this traditional understanding of 'penal substitution'. Some have suggested that Jesus bore the pain or weight of our sin rather than

1 Peter 2:24 ☐

Hebrews 9:28 ☐

the penalty due to our sin; while others have maintained that Jesus took our place simply by offering a perfect confession of our sins.

We must keep on affirming the church's traditional understanding of 'penal substitution', because Jesus did endure and exhaust the destructive divine judgement (which was ours by right) to win our eternal salvation.

We should, however, also recognise that 'pain-bearing substitution' and 'penitent substitution' do have a place in the biblical picture of salvation – and we can see this most clearly in the ritual associated with the Jewish Day of Atonement.

It is true that, on the cross, as the substitute, Jesus bore what humanity could not bear – the righteous punishment of sin – and this is fundamental to salvation. But it is also true (though not fundamental) that he offered what humanity would not offer – a complete confession of its sin; and that he endured what we could not endure – the full pain and hurt of every evil thought and action since the Garden of Eden.

The Day of Atonement

The concept of 'sin-bearing' is found in the many Old Testament passages which describe innocent people suffering the consequences of someone else's guilt: for example, Exodus 28:43; Leviticus 5:17; 19:8; 22:9; 24:15; Numbers 9:13; 14:34; 18:22; 30:15 & Lamentations 5:7.

But the same language of sin-bearing is also used when God himself provides the substitute – as in Leviticus 10:17 and Ezekiel 4:4–5. This important idea is particularly clear in the ritual associated with the annual Day of Atonement – which is described in Leviticus 16.

The Day of Atonement was a once-a-year *corporate* or national sacrifice for sin – in contrast to the regular *personal* sacrifices for sin. It was the most important day in the Jewish year, and the only occasion when 'the holy of holies' was entered, and then only by the high priest.

The high priest took two male goats to atone for – to cover – all the sins of the whole people of Israel. He slaughtered one goat, and sprinkled its blood on the altar in the usual fashion. He then placed both his hands on the other goat's head, confessed all the wickedness and rebellion of God's people, and drove the goat away into the desert so that it would symbolically 'bear' their sins away.

Margin references:
Exodus 28:43 ☐
Leviticus 5:17 ☐
19:8 ☐
22:9 ☐
24:15 ☐
Numbers 9:13 ☐
14:34 ☐
18:22 ☐
30:15 ☐
Lamentations 5:7 ☐
Leviticus 10:17 ☐
Ezekiel 4:4–5 ☐
Leviticus 16 ☐

Leviticus 16:5 shows that the two goats were *a single sacrifice*: each embodied different aspects of the same sacrifice. The great and abiding revelation of the Day of Atonement was that reconciliation was possible only through a single substitutionary sacrifice which involved sin-bearing.

We also need to recognise that the atoning process involved:

- *a substitutionary confession by the high priest*
- *a substitutionary pain-bearing or load-bearing by the scape-goat*
- *a substitutionary penalty-bearing by the sacrificed goat*

The book of Hebrews identifies Jesus as the high priest and as both goats – we see this in Hebrews 2:17; 9:7, 12, 28. This underlines the slightly wider understanding of substitution that we have suggested.

Isaiah 53

Although the two goats had a sin-bearing role, it must have been clear to many Jews that an animal was an inadequate substitute for a human. As we have seen, Isaiah's four 'servant songs' soon introduced the gentle servant of God who would suffer, bear sin and die for people.

The servant's suffering and death are described in Isaiah 53: no other Old Testament passage is as important to the New Testament as this.

Verses 1, 4, 5, 6, 7, 8, 9 and 11 are directly referred to in John 12:38; Matthew 8:17; 1 Peter 2:22–25 and Acts 8:30–35. And every verse except 2 is alluded to somewhere in the New Testament: for example, vs. 3 – Mark 9:12; vs. 7 – Mark 14:61; 15:5; Luke 23:9; John 19:9; vs. 8 – Mark 2:20; vs. 9 – Mark 14:8; vs. 10 – John 10:11, 15, 17; vs. 11 – Matthew 3:15; vs. 12 – Luke 11:22; 22:37; 23:34.

It is beyond dispute that Isaiah 53 is basic both to the New Testament understanding of Jesus *and* to Jesus' understanding of himself. Jesus' words in Mark 10:45 and 14:24 directly refer to Isaiah 53:12 and demonstrate that he understood his death as a sin-bearing death.

The whole thrust of Isaiah 53 is *substitutionary* and *sacrificial*. It reveals that the Suffering Servant:

- *bore our griefs* – verse 4
- *carried our sorrows* – verse 4

- *was wounded for our transgressions* – verse 5
- *was bruised for our iniquities* – verse 5
- *was chastised for our peace* – verse 5
- *was whipped for our healing* – verse 5
- *carried our iniquities* – verse 6
- *was stricken for our transgressions* – verse 8
- *bore our iniquities* – verse 11
- *bore our sin* – verse 12

Isaiah 53:4–6 are convincing proof that God's Servant is a substitute whose sacrifice involves bearing *both* the 'penalty' of sin and the 'pain' of sin.

Jesus died *for* us

The wide sweep of Old Testament teaching about sacrifices and substitutes prepares the way for, and helps us to understand correctly, the New Testament teaching that Jesus died for human beings. We see this, for example, in Matthew 20:28; Mark 10:45; Romans 5:6–8; 14:15; 1 Corinthians 8:11; 15:3; 2 Corinthians 5:14–15; 1 Thessalonians 5:10 and 1 Timothy 2:6.

There are over 40 different Greek prepositions which can be translated as the single English word 'for', and some scholars make much of a subtle difference between two of them. *Hyper* means 'for' in the broad sense of 'on behalf of', while *anti* means 'for' in the narrow sense of 'instead of'.

Most of the passages which describe Christ dying 'for' people use *hyper* (only Matthew 20:28 and Mark 10:45 use *anti*) and some teachers use this to support their belief that Christ's death was merely representative rather than fully substitutionary.

This idea, however, ignores the wider biblical teaching about substitutional sacrifices and overlooks the fact that the broad sense of *hyper* includes the narrow sense of *anti*. In fact, the New Testament writers often use *hyper* in a context which clearly means 'instead of' – for example, 2 Corinthians 5:20 and Philemon 1:13.

Hyper is used in the three strongest New Testament statements about Christ's death – 2 Corinthians 5:21, Galatians 3:13 and 1 Timothy 2:6.

In these verses, Paul explains that Christ's death was intended to benefit us – in this sense it was 'on our behalf'. But 2 Corinthians 5:21 must also mean that Jesus bore the penalty of our sin 'instead of us', and Galatians 3:13 must mean that the curse of the Law lying on us was transferred to him so that he bore it 'instead of us'.

These verses show that a mysterious exchange takes place when we are united to Christ. He takes our curse so that we might receive his blessing; he becomes sin with our sin so that we may become righteous with his righteousness.

The apostle Paul calls this exchange 'imputation' in, for example, Romans 4:6; 1 Corinthians 1:30 and Philippians 3:9. It is important we recognise that this imputation involves the acceptance of legal consequences rather than the transference of moral qualities (though these qualities do grow within us through the work of the Holy Spirit).

Our state of inner sinfulness was not transferred to Jesus to make him personally sinful, and his moral perfection was not transferred to us to make us personally perfect. Instead, on the cross, as the substitute, Jesus voluntarily accepted the liability or consequence of our sins – this is what the Bible means by the phrases 'made sin' and 'made a curse'.

Similarly, 'the righteousness of God' which is imputed to us when we are 'in Christ' is not an instant righteousness of character and conduct, it is an instant righteous standing before God. We receive Christ's righteousness so that we can stand with impunity and joy before God.

THE SUBSTITUTE

In *Knowing the Father* and *Knowing the Spirit*, we see how important it is to understand correctly the nature of the triune God; and in *Knowing the Son* we consider in some detail the full nature of Jesus. Quite simply, we will never understand the cross correctly until we grasp the natures of the Father, the Son and the Spirit.

Most of the secular objections to the cross are based on wrong ideas about God and Christ; and nearly all the Christian misunderstandings about salvation come from inaccurate pictures of the relationship between the Father and the Son.

The idea of substitution rests on the identity of the substitute. Everyone knows that Christ was the substitute, but we need to grasp precisely who the Christ is who died on the cross.

An independent Jesus

Unbelievers think that the person who died on the cross was simply a human being. Although most Christians reject this idea for the reasons we set out in *Knowing the Son*, many believers think that the Son was an individual being who was quite separate from God – an independent third party in the act of salvation.

This means that they present the cross either as Jesus trying to pacify an angry God and grasp a begrudging salvation, or as an unjust God who kills an innocent Jesus in place of the real culprits.

We establish in *Knowing the Father* that this is a grievous misrepresentation of the Father. He is not reluctant to suffer himself or to forgive humanity, and he is not a cold tyrant whose anger has to be appeased and whose antipathy to humanity has to be overcome by someone outside himself, by some third party.

This 'third party' approach sets the Son against the Father, yet there has never been any discord or conflict between them. Whatever happened on the cross was willed and accepted by both equally.

The second clause of Isaiah 53:10 is notoriously difficult to translate. It is unclear in Hebrew who makes the offering: the clause could mean either 'though God offers his servant as an offering' or 'though the servant offers himself as an offering'.

At first sight, the New Testament appears to be equally ambiguous. Passages like Mark 14:27; John 3:16; Romans 3:25; 4:25; 8:3, 32 and 2 Corinthians 5:21 stress that the Father sacrificed the Son.

Whereas Matthew 20:28; Galatians 2:20; Ephesians 5:2, 25; 1 Timothy 2:6; Titus 2:14 and Hebrews 9:14, 26 emphasise that the Son sacrificed himself.

Isaiah 53:10 ☐

Mark 14:27 ☐

John 3:16 ☐

Romans 3:25 ☐
4:25 ☐
8:3, 32 ☐

2 Corinthians 5:21 ☐

Matthew 20:28 ☐

Galatians 2:20 ☐

Ephesians 5:2, 25 ☐

1 Timothy 2:6 ☐

Titus 2:14 ☐

Hebrews 9:14, 26 ☐

SUBSTITUTION AND SACRIFICE

Once again, the truth is *parallel and inter-related*. The Father gave the Son and the Son freely gave himself. The Father sacrificed his Son, and the Son voluntarily sacrificed himself. The Father did not make the Son endure an ordeal he was unwilling to bear, and the Son did not surprise the Father by his selfless action. Galatians 1:4 and John 10:17–18 express this paradox very plainly.

Galatians 1:4
John 10:17–18

In one sense, the story of Abraham and Isaac on Mount Moriah is an obvious foreshadowing, for there we see the father ready to sacrifice his favourite son, and the son prepared to be the willing victim. At another level, however, it is a thoroughly inadequate picture because Abraham and Isaac are separate, independent beings.

We have seen throughout this *Sword of the Spirit* series that God is not divided into three. He is one, but more than one. The Father, the Son and The Spirit are not three distinct individuals; they are three self-distinctions within one being who reveal their essential oneness in a three-fold diversity of 'uni-persons', characteristics and functions.

If we misunderstand this absolute divine unity we are likely to fall into error whenever we think about the cross. If we think of the Father and the Son as separate individuals we inevitably caricature Calvary as either God punishing an innocent Jesus or as Jesus persuading a reluctant Father.

But 2 Corinthians 5:18–19 makes it clear that the sacrifice was not made by Christ alone, or by God alone, but by God acting in-and-through Christ with his full agreement. They worked together in harmony. Their functions may have been different but their wills were one. They were co-dependent not independent.

2 Corinthians 5:18–19

God himself

The essential unity of God has led some people (they are usually called 'Unitarians') to believe that God alone was the substitute, that he took our place and died for us.

They argue: 1 Corinthians 2:8 shows that it was the Lord of Glory who was crucified; Revelation reveals that the Lamb who died is at the centre of God's throne; Hebrews 9:17 teaches that we can benefit from the promises in a will only after the testator has died; and Acts 20:28 announces that God purchased the church with his own blood.

1 Corinthians 2:8
Hebrews 9:17
Acts 20:28

Their argument fails, however on the fact that no verse specifically declares that God himself died on the cross, and on the realisation that the immortality of God means he could not have died.

Common sense should be enough to convince us that God simply had to become human (without ceasing to be God or becoming independent of God) if he was to die as our substitute and simultaneously be both Judge and innocent victim. Hebrews 2:14–18 and Philippians 2:6–8 state this particularly clearly.

We note in *Knowing the Father* that the New Testament usually means 'the first uni-person of God, the Father' when it mentions God. This is another reason why it can be misleading to suggest that 'God' died on the cross – for it was the fully-human, fully-divine Son who died, not the fully-divine Father.

If we over-emphasise 'God's' sufferings on the cross we are in danger of confusing the 'uni-persons' of the Trinity, of denying the eternal distinctiveness of the Son, and of denying Jesus' full humanity.

Passages like Romans 5:12–19; Galatians 4:4; Philippians 2:7–8 and Hebrews 5:8 underline the 'unity *and* functional distinctiveness' within God by stressing the Son's willing submission to the Father. As we see in *Knowing the Son*, this is the essence of Jesus' sonship.

God-in-Christ

The substitute who took our place, offered our full confession, bore the pain of all our sin, and endured the penalty incurred by all our rebellious disobedience was not Christ alone (as this would make him an outside third party) or God alone (because this would negate the incarnation).

Instead, the Substitute on the cross was *God-in-Christ*, fully-human and fully-divine, uniquely qualified to represent both God and humanity, and to mediate between them.

Whenever we think about the cross in terms of Christ suffering and dying, we overlook the Father's gracious initiative. But when we think about it in terms of God suffering and dying, we overlook the Son's gracious mediation.

In contrast to these partial approaches, the New Testament consistently stresses that the Father acted in salvation 'in-and-through Christ with his whole-hearted agreement'. We see this, for example, in Matthew 1:1–23; Mark 14:36; Luke 2:11; John 4:34; 6:38–39; 8:29; 10:18, 30; 14:11; 15:10; 17:4, 21–23; 19:30; 2 Corinthians 5:17–19; Colossians 1:19–20; 2:9 and Hebrews 10:7.

It should be obvious that only a human *should* make atonement for the sins of humanity (because it is men and women who have sinned) and that only God *could* make the necessary atonement (since it is he who had justly demanded it).

Jesus Christ, therefore is the only possible substitute because he is the only person in whom the *should* and *could* are united by virtue of his fully-human, fully-divine nature.

The cross

These ideas of 'divine oneness' and 'God-in-Christ' mean, first, that there are only two participants in the drama of the cross, not three: humanity and God; and, second, that it is all down to grace.

In giving his Son, God graciously gave himself for us. In sending the Son, he graciously came himself for us. By grace, the Judge intervened and himself endured the penalty that he had imposed on us. In order to save sinful humanity in a way which was fully consistent with his holy nature, God-in Christ graciously substituted himself for us.

All that we have examined in Parts Two and Three should convince us that 'divine self-consistency through divine substitution' is the only possible explanation of the cross. Before we move on to consider what happened on the cross, and its consequences and implications for us, we need to be absolutely clear what the cross is and is not.

For example, the cross was not:

- *a bargain with the devil*
- *a requirement of some code of law or honour*
- *a punishment of an innocent Jesus by a harsh Father*
- *a means of extracting salvation from a mean Father*
- *an action of the Father which by-passed Christ's mediation*

Instead, the just-and-loving God humbled himself to become – in-and-through his only Son – human flesh, and to endure and accept

---

Matthew 1:1–23 ☐
Mark 14:36 ☐
Luke 2:11 ☐
John 4:34 ☐
     6:38–39 ☐
     8:29 ☐
     10:18, 30 ☐
     14:11 ☐
     15:10 ☐
     17:4 ☐
     17:21–23 ☐
     19:30 ☐
2 Corinthians
     5:17–19 ☐
Colossians
     1:19–20 ☐
     2:9 ☐
Hebrews 10:7 ☐

the terrible consequences of human sin. He graciously did this so that he could save us without compromising his holy divine character.

In many ways, substitution is at the heart of both sin and salvation. We can say that the essence of sin is humanity substituting itself for God, while the essence of salvation is God substituting himself for humanity.

Through our rebellious sin, we put ourselves where only God should be; and by his amazing grace, God puts himself where only we deserve to be. Truly our salvation is by grace.

PART FOUR

covenants of grace

During the 'Last Supper', when Jesus and his apostles had gathered together to eat the Passover meal, Jesus took a loaf of bread, gave thanks for it, broke it into pieces, and handed it round with the words recorded in Matthew 26:26–28; Mark 14:2–24; Luke 22:17–19 and 1 Corinthians 11:23–25.

In the same way, after the meal, Jesus took a cup of wine, gave thanks for it, passed it to them, and said, 'This cup is the new covenant in my blood', and, 'This is my blood of the new covenant, which is poured out for many for the forgiveness of sins'.

We consider the communion meal which Jesus instituted in *Glory in the Church*, and examine its roots in the family Passover celebration. Here, however, we need to grasp Jesus' important assertion that, through the shedding of his blood in death, God was taking the initiative to establish a 'new covenant' or a 'fresh binding agreement' with his people which promised forgiveness.

If we are to understand the 'new covenant' accurately, we need to consider the 'old covenants' which preceded and foreshadowed Jesus' death on the cross.

Matthew 26:26–28 ☐

Mark 14:2–24 ☐

Luke 22:17–19 ☐

1 Corinthians 11:23–25 ☐

OLD COVENANTS

Genesis 6:18

Genesis 6:18 records the first mention of a covenant, and lays down many of the most important biblical principles of covenant. God took the initiative and made a binding agreement with Noah which promised salvation by grace. It was not a contract between God and Noah which benefited both parties, it was all grace, all God, all for Noah's family's benefit and salvation in a time of judgement.

God simply announced to Noah that he would establish his covenant with him. It was God's covenant, he established it; it was a sovereign dispensation of saving grace from-and-by God to Noah and his family.

Even though the covenant was all-grace, Noah's family had to respond by entering the ark to experience the benefits of covenant salvation. We can say that the covenant was all-grace, but that Noah's family had to appropriate the promise by faith-filled obedience.

The covenant with Noah

Genesis 9:9–17

After the Flood had subsided, God repeated his covenant promise to Noah and his family. Genesis 9:9–17 describes what happened, and reveals even more clearly the essential nature of God's covenants.

Once again, there was no 'bi-lateral agreement'; it was plainly all grace, all God's initiative and action, all for Noah's family's benefit. We can say that this old covenant was:

- *willed, initiated and established entirely by God himself*

- *universal in scope; it embraced not only Noah but also his descendants – this proves that the giving of grace is not dependent on a favourable response by the beneficiaries*

- *unconditional; there were no pre-conditions or requirements – in fact there were even no on-going obligations, which shows that it was impossible for the covenant to be broken*

- *accompanied by a confirming sign; the rainbow could not be controlled or manipulated by humanity, and was God's guarantee of his faithfulness*

- *everlasting; there is never any uncertainty about an unconditional promise*

The covenant with Abram

God spoke to Abram in Genesis 12:1–3, and Abram responded in faith by leaving Haran for Canaan.

Many years later, God confirmed his word to Abram in Genesis 15:1. But this time, in 15:2–3, Abram questioned God about the way the promise would be fulfilled. God replied to Abram in verses 4–5, and – through seeing the stars in the sky – Abram 'saw' God's promise to him and believed.

Verse 6 reports that Abram put his faith in God and that this was credited to him as righteousness. Even so, Abram wanted to be 100% sure that God's promise would be fulfilled, and – in verse 8 – he asked God for a guarantee of assurance, for a sign which would confirm God's word to him. In reality, he was asking God to enter into a binding agreement with him.

God responded by establishing the covenant which is described in verses 9–21. This resembles the ancient covenantal rituals described in Jeremiah 34:18: in these, both contracting parties passed between the parts of the slaughtered animals and called down on themselves the fate of the sacrificial victim should they break the agreement.

In this case, however, God alone passed between the animal parts to show that his covenants are always unilateral pacts: they are exclusively and entirely all-grace initiatives. The flame in the story is *Yahweh* himself, as in Exodus 3:2; 13:21 and 19:18. The darkness and length of time foreshadow Calvary when God would make a similar covenant through the shed blood and broken body of Jesus.

In this blood covenant with Abram, God was saying, 'Let me be as these broken pieces of animals if I fail to fulfil my word to you.' The covenant anticipated (it prepared the way for) the oath that God made in Genesis 22:16–17 at the completion of Abraham's faith.

This old covenant helps us to understand that Christ's blood on the cross is God's solemn pledge that he will keep his new covenant promise of forgiveness to us.

The blood is a God-given aid to faith, the assurance that we need because of our weakness. We should also be able to see how the blood also anticipates God's oath to us, his 'rainbow' in our lives – the anointing of the Spirit on our lives.

Genesis 12:1–3 ☐

Genesis 15:1–21 ☐

Jeremiah 34:18 ☐

Exodus 3:2 ☐
13:21 ☐
19:18 ☐

Genesis 22:16–17 ☐

The covenant with Israel

Some church traditions maintain that this covenant is very different from the other covenants, and that it is a covenant of 'works' rather than 'grace'. But passages like Exodus 2:24; 3:16; 6:4–8; Psalms 105:8–12, 42–45; 106:45 show that all God's dealings with Israel were based on the promise of his binding agreement with Abram.

Just as God's covenants with Noah and Abraham were declared in several stages, so he also made one covenant with his people through Moses in several stages. The details of the stages may differ, but the principles of grace and promise run through them all.

We should appreciate that:

- God's covenant in Exodus 19:5; 24:1–18; 34:1–35; Deuteronomy 29:1–29 was made with a people which had already been *chosen*, *redeemed*, *created* and *adopted* by the sovereign grace of God.

  We see this in Exodus 2:25; 4:22–23; 6:6–8; 15:13; 20:2; Deuteronomy 4:37; 7:6–8; 8:5, 17–18; 9:4–6, 26; 13:5; 14:1–2; 21:8; 32:6; 1 Chronicles 29:10; Isaiah 63:16; 64:8; Jeremiah 3:19; 31:9; Hosea 9:1; 13:5; Amos 3:2; Malachi 1:6 and 2:10.

- The same spiritual relationship which was at the heart of the covenants with Noah and Abram was also at the centre of the covenant with Israel – Exodus 6:7; Deuteronomy 29:10–13.

- God's gracious sovereign initiative was at the forefront of the covenant – Exodus 19:5–8; 24: 3–4; Deuteronomy 4:13–14.

God's agreement with Israel is often called a covenant of 'law' or 'works' because there is so much scriptural emphasis on Israel's obedience to the law – which was an addition to God's basic promise to Abraham. God's people would now be blessed whenever they obeyed the law and cursed whenever they disobeyed.

This obligation of obedience, however, was – in principle – similar to the obligations that God gave in Genesis 6:18–22; 17:9–14 and 18:18–19. And none of the obligations were pre-conditions of their respective covenants, there were simply the means of appropriating and enjoying the blessings of the covenant.

By grace, God's successive covenants created the possibility of his people living in a covenant relationship with him. Since God is holy, those who enter into a relationship with him are called to live in-and-with his holiness. We see this in Deuteronomy 6:4–15; Leviticus 11:44–45; 19:2; 20:7, 26; 21:8 – and in 1 Peter 1:15; Hebrews 12:14.

Some believers interpret Exodus 19:5–6 and 24:7–8 to mean that the covenant with Israel did not begin until the people had promised to obey the Law. But the covenant had begun back with Abram, and the Law was simply an addition to this pre-existing covenant.

The people knew that God was a covenant-keeping God because he had delivered them from Egypt. They knew that the covenant was already in operation; that the grace had been given and received; that the agreement between God and the children of Abraham already existed. Now, however, the Law was being added to the covenant.

This means that the Jew's promise of obedience in Exodus 24:7 was not their way into the covenant, it was their commitment to living in the covenant by the Law. It was their response to the grace of God.

Throughout this *Sword of the Spirit* series, we stress that, as believers in the new covenant, we are called to 'gospel obedience' – a 'particular, enabled obedience to the personal rule of God'. Although the type of obedience in the new covenant is wonderfully different to the 'legal obedience' of the old covenant, we must realise that the obligation of obedience in the new covenant is, in principle, the same obligation which has featured in all God's covenants.

As we see in Parts Five to Eight, although every aspect of the new covenant is an accomplished fact, we do not enjoy the full blessings of the covenant *on earth* without perseverance and loving obedience.

The messianic covenant

Although the word 'covenant' is not used in 2 Samuel 7:12–17, it is obvious from passages like Psalm 89:3–4, 26–37 and 132:11–18 that this is God's binding agreement with David.

Once again, it is plain that this is entirely a work of grace which binds God to his unilateral promise and guarantees the promise to the beneficiaries. We see this in, for example, Psalm 89:3 and 2 Samuel 23:5.

This 'final' manifestation of an old covenant is the clearest foreshadowing of the new covenant in-and-through Jesus, for it plainly points to the Messiah. We see this in Isaiah 42:1–6; 49:8; 55:3–4; Malachi 3:1; Luke 1:32–33 and Acts 2:30–36.

The Isaiah passages reveal that 'the Servant' (whom we considered in Part Three) is himself 'the covenant' because the blessings and provisions of God's covenant with his people are so bound up in the Messiah that he is actually the embodiment of the blessings and the presence of God which the covenant ensures.

This biblical overview of the old covenants should be enough to convince us that God deals with his people through covenants, and of:

- *the richness of his covenantal grace*
- *the certainty of his covenantal provision*
- *the assurance of his covenantal promises*

THE NEW COVENANT

When we read Jesus' announcement that his blood is the blood of the covenant shed for the forgiveness of sins, and that the cup of the Last Supper is the new covenant in his blood, we can understand his words correctly only within the context of biblical covenants.

Without reading a page of the New Testament, we can guess that a new covenant will be an act of all-grace, that it will provide significant blessings, guarantee important promises, establish a holy relationship between God and his people, and demand some form of obedience.

The New Testament teaches that the new covenant fulfilled the old covenants and brought them to fruition. The grace which was partially revealed in the old covenants was fully revealed and given. The relationship which was partially enjoyed in the old covenants was brought to the greatest possible degree of intimacy. The blessings of the old covenants were developed, increased, intensified, supplemented, perfected, and so on.

We can see this in Galatians 3:15–22, where the apostle Paul stresses that the covenant with Israel did not cancel the covenant with Abram. He explains that the later covenant was an addition, not a suspension, which served the basic covenant promise of relationship; and he shows that the two covenants were based on the same basic principles of grace promise and human faith.

As later covenants supplement earlier covenants, Galatians 3:15–16 presents Christ as the fulfilment of the covenant promise made to Abram. Luke 1:72 also reports Zacharias' prophecy that the redemptive work of Jesus will fulfil God's covenant with Abram.

Although we know that the new covenant refers essentially to the new relationship established through Jesus' broken body on the cross, we can be sure that the new covenant also encapsulates all the saving grace, blessing, truth and promises of all the old covenants.

2 Corinthians 3:6–18 describes some of the new benefits of the new covenant: it ministers righteousness, liberty, and the Spirit of life; and it begins the process by which (by gospel obedience) we are transformed into the holy image of God by the Holy Spirit of the Lord.

We have seen that God's covenants with his people are always unilateral, binding agreements of grace and promise, and that they are always set in-and-around the context of salvation and redemption.

From the time of Noah until today, God's saving grace and certain blessings have always been given in the form of covenants. Each successive covenant has unfolded more of God's redemptive will and purpose, yet none has deviated from the central and governing features of all the covenants. Each successive covenant has always been an additional enrichment of what has always been present.

We know that Calvary is the climax of grace, promise, redemption, revelation and relationship; but we must not forget that the eternal covenant promise, 'I will be your God and you will be my people', is at the centre of the cross. The new covenant through the blood of Christ brings this relationship to the highest possible level. Quite simply, there can never be a greater promise or a more intimate relationship than that which has been graciously provided by the new covenant.

BLOOD COVENANTS

We have seen that the New Testament, especially Galatians 3, looks back to God's blood covenant with Abram as the foundation of Christian faith, and that it establishes the new covenant of the blood on the basis of the Abramic covenant of grace, promise and faith.

God's Genesis 15:17–18 blood covenant with Abram developed the grace already revealed in the covenant with Noah. God made no demands, and Abram offered no promises. These come later, in 17:1 and 22:12, as God called Abram into a closer relationship and holier lifestyle, but the blood covenant itself was an occasion of pure grace.

Abram's lapses were not mentioned, and did not hinder the covenant. The covenant was made after Abram had shown faith and before Abram's obedience was requested, tested and confirmed. Exactly the same all-grace principle was followed in the blood covenant at Calvary.

When 1 Corinthians 11:25 and Hebrews 8:6–10 describe the cross in terms of a new covenant, they mean that 'the blood' is God's pledge to humanity. God had never broken his Genesis 15 promise, yet he let what happened to the animals then happen to himself at Calvary.

At the cross, there was no demand for obedience, only an offer of forgiveness. Our lapses and doubt did not hinder the covenant, for it was another occasion of pure all-grace.

Since the new blood covenant on the cross, there is nothing more that God can do. He has made his unconditional, everlasting promise, and the blood witnesses to God's total sincerity and faithfulness. The blood now binds God to keep his word for all eternity.

The blood of Christ

Some sections of the church focus on Christ's blood, and make much use of terms like, 'washed in the blood', 'covered by the blood', 'promised through the blood' and 'guaranteed by the blood'.

'The blood' literally refers to the blood which poured from Jesus at the cross, but most believers use it as short-hand for the complete sacrificial death of Jesus. We can say that 'the blood' represents the totality of Christ's death, and is God's pledge of the new covenant.

Paul's letter to the Romans contains the Bible's clearest and most detailed explanation of salvation. Paul uses many contemporary word-pictures (like 'justification', 'redemption', 'propitiation') to describe the results of Christ's death – and we consider these in Part Five.

In chapter 5, Paul begins with his great theme of justification by faith, explains that Christ died in our place, and then shows that the great purpose of this was that we might be reconciled with God.

COVENANTS OF GRACE

As we see in *Reaching the Lost*, reconciliation is not one aspect of salvation, it is the great over-riding purpose of salvation. We are redeemed, justified and forgiven *so that* we can be reconciled with God. And it is the blood of Jesus, shed in his faith-filled substitutionary death, which both accomplishes and evidences our reconciliation.

The New Testament teaches that the blood of Jesus performed what the ritual sacrifices of the Old Testament could only symbolise and the old covenants could only foreshadow – eternal forgiveness from sin.

Sacrificial blood

We have seen that, at Passover, the blood of a sacrificial animal – it could be a male lamb or goat – was sprinkled in faith on the door-posts of Jewish homes as a sign that they were God's covenant people.

When God saw the blood, he passed over the house and did not destroy the first-born when his wrath visited Egypt. This is why Jesus is called the 'Passover lamb', for it is through our faith in his covenant blood that God passes over us and does not punish us for our sin.

We have also seen that, on the Day of the Atonement, a bull was sacrificed for the sin of the High Priest and his family, and two goats were sacrificed for the guilt and sin of the people. The blood of the bull and the sacrificial goat were then sprinkled by the High Priest on-and-before the mercy-seat and altar as an act of atonement for the uncleanness and rebellion of the Israelites.

In the same way, Jesus' death is recognised throughout the New Testament as essentially a sacrifice for human sin. We see this, for example, in 1 Corinthians 5:7; 2 Corinthians 5:14; Galatians 2:20; Ephesians 5:2; Hebrews 5–10; 1 Peter 3:18 and 1 John 2:2.

This means that the blood is the evidence and assurance of the death of a sacrifice, *and* the pledge of God's covenant. The New Testament identifies ten ways that 'the blood' assures us of God's new covenant with us. We can confidently say that the blood guarantees our:

1. *forgiveness* – Ephesians 1:7
2. *cleansing* – 1 John 1:7
3. *righteousness* – Romans 5:9
4. *redemption* – Ephesians 1:7

1 Corinthians 5:7 ☐
2 Corinthians 5:14 ☐
Galatians 2:20 ☐
Ephesians 5:2 ☐
Hebrews 5–10 ☐
1 Peter 3:18 ☐
1 John 2:2 ☐

Ephesians 1:7 ☐
1 John 1:7 ☐
Romans 5:9 ☐
Ephesians 1:7 ☐

5. *sanctification* – Hebrews 10:10; 13:12

6. *purchase* – 1 Corinthians 6:19–20

7. *deliverance from the curse of the Law* – Galatians 3:13

8. *promised inheritance* – Hebrews 9:15–18

9. *freedom from inherited bondages* – 1 Peter 1:18–19

10. *victory over Satan* – Colossians 2:15; Hebrews 2:14; John 12:31–33

All these covenant promises are summarised, and implicitly referred to, in the phrase, 'the blood of Christ'. His blood is the visible guarantee of all these achievements. This means that we must believe in a God of blood sacrifice and blood covenants; and that we must consider 'the blood' as not only central to Scripture but as also at the heart of God's covenant nature.

We see this in Romans 3:24–26 and 5:8, and can say that 'the blood' is the ultimate assurance of God's all-grace nature *and* of faith in the God who revealed himself through his blood as infinitely gracious.

A sign of love

The New Testament always defines love in terms of God's sacrifice on the cross, for example, Romans 5:8; 1 John 3:15–20 and 4:7–21.

At the cross, God gave everything because of his love for those who deserve nothing. The Father gave the Son for those who prefer to worship other gods; the Son gave himself for those who steadfastly ignore him; and they both surrendered their relationship with each other because of their unimaginable love for us all.

Since the Calvary blood sacrifice, nobody can look at a cross and question God's love – because nothing reveals God's love more clearly than 'the blood'. Quite simply, the blood proves for all eternity that God loves us, and has embraced us as his covenant people.

This means we can say that Christ's blood is the assurance of:

- *who God is*
- *what God has done for us in salvation*
- *all the covenant blessings*

A token of assurance

We see in *Living Faith* that we have been given a double guarantee of our faith: God's word *and* the blood of the new covenant. And we have noted here that all the covenant promises are pledged by the new covenant blood.

This means that God's promises to us are now enshrined in a covenant which was both made in Jesus' blood *and* put into effect by his blood. We see this in Hebrews 9:20 and Romans 8:32. (The context of these two passages helps us to appreciate that the blood also deals with the consequences of our failure and places us in a victorious position over our enemy. We consider this in Part Seven.)

Hebrews 9:27–28 makes it plain that Christ's blood completely deals with everything – all our sin, guilt, doubts, weaknesses and failings. The first coming of Christ had a direct relationship to sin, as we see in Romans 8:3 and 2 Corinthians 5:21, but his second coming will have no connection with sin because redemption, by the blood, has been completed. As Jesus said on the cross, it really is 'finished'.

Romans 8:34–39, perhaps the high-point of the whole New Testament, shows that the blood, the death of Christ, guarantees that we are in a triumphant position over death and demons, over the present and the future, over all heavenly powers. This means that the covenant blood of Christ guarantees our covenant relationship: nothing can ever separate us from the love of God, which we know in Christ Jesus. This is the unsurpassable new covenant relationship which is ours by grace.

The covenant blood of Christ is the final assurance of faith. It is the ultimate guarantee that *Yahweh* is who he is, that he has become on the cross what we need in order to satisfy his self-consistency and reconcile us with him for all eternity.

Once we know that our sin has been dealt with by the blood, that our conscience has been cleansed by the blood, and that our guilt has been removed by the blood, we are eternally secure – for his covenant can never be broken.

Sidebar references:
- Hebrews 9:20 ☐
- Romans 8:32 ☐
- Hebrews 9:27–28 ☐
- Romans 8:3 ☐
- 2 Corinthians 5:21 ☐
- Romans 8:34–39 ☐

PART FIVE

salvation and atonement

We have seen that the Old and New Testaments are united in their common record of God's all-grace initiative in saving a people for himself according to his unbreakable covenants. The three great scriptural themes of 'the people of God', 'the salvation of God' and 'the victory of God' are woven from Genesis to Revelation.

In both Testaments, salvation:

- *is initiated and accomplished by God's grace alone*
- *is received by faith*
- *operates objectively within history and human lives*
- *is costly to God*
- *involves a rescue from enemies*
- *brings wholeness to body and spirit*
- *produces spiritual triumph*
- *reveals God's love*
- *vindicates human faith*

But both Testaments are not the same, for the Old is always looking forward, always preparing the way for the New. It looks to God to re-enact in the future his great acts of judgement and grace from the past.

For example, the Old looks forward to a more glorious David, Moses, Elijah and Melchizedek, to an exodus whose deliverance would be even greater, to an even more awesome Passover, to a better temple, to a new creation, to an ultimate covenant, and so on. And what the Old hoped for, the New declares has been fulfilled in Christ.

New Testament salvation

Most of the New Testament teaching on salvation matches with the Old Testament understanding; differences arise only where the ideas are deepened, internalised, spiritualised and personalised in Jesus' sacrificial death. In fact, we can say that the New Testament enlarges the Old Testament experience of salvation without contradicting it.

One difference between the Testaments is the New's teaching that the enemy from which we are saved is spiritual rather than physical. No longer are we saved from pagan nations, now we are saved from the *old age* (sin, law, sickness, wrath and death), the *old condition* (conformity to a godless world), the *old fears* (despair, depression and dread), the *old habits* (agreement with the pattern of sinful worldliness), and the *old foe* (Satan himself).

But the most important difference is that the New Testament gathers every aspect of salvation in a single world-changing event – the substitutionary death of Jesus Christ on the cross of Calvary. Although, in many ways, the cross is merely the natural consequence and consummation of all God's dealings in grace and judgement since Eden, it is almost impossible to exaggerate the greatness of the changes that it accomplished – both in God and in us, and especially in our relationship with him. In fact, we can say that a completely new age dawned when Christ died and was raised from death.

2 Corinthians 6:2 describes this new age as 'the day of salvation', and the magnificent covenant blessings of this great salvation are so diverse that they cannot be defined neatly.

In *Glory in the Church* we see that the New Testament uses a whole host of pictures to describe the mystery of the church. These are

2 Corinthians 6:2 ☐

'parallel' or 'complementary' images: although it is hard to see how the church can simultaneously be both the body of Christ and the bride of Christ, we know that the pictures come together in the truth that God is calling out and gathering together a people for himself.

It is much the same with salvation. The New Testament uses many different ideas about, and images of, salvation to help us understand the fullness of the cross and the magnitude of its accomplishments, and it is important that we try to grasp them all and hold them together.

Underlying all the ideas and images, however, is the single truth that, in his grace, God has sent his Son as the substitute to bear our sin and die our death, to satisfy God's self-consistency, to deliver us from sin and death, and to reconcile us with himself for all eternity.

JESUS' UNIQUE MISSION

In *Knowing the Son* we consider Jesus' unique mission and learn why the Father sent Jesus into the world.

We see that he was sent to break the power of evil and death, for Satan had taken authority on earth and the world was under his sway. So Jesus willingly came into the world to establish the kingdom of God, disarm the evil powers of darkness, and triumph over them.

But Jesus was also sent to reach the lost; he was sent to save hurting people who were powerless to save themselves. So, at great personal sacrifice, he came to make atonement – to be the substitute for every member of humanity, to bear the wrath of God against sin, to reconcile man and women to each other and God.

As well as this, the Father sent the Son to demonstrate a life of perfect submission and consecration, to be the pattern and example for people of all ages and races. So, in his daily death to self and the desires of the flesh, Jesus came to show us how we should live and die.

And Jesus was also sent to show the world what God is like, to reveal and reproduce the glorious Father's nature. So he came as God's living Word, as a unique and complete revelation of the invisible God, to reproduce the divine nature in humanity.

Each aspect of Jesus' ministry reached its fulfilment at Calvary. Although the cross was a simple event which accomplished the single objective of our salvation, it was also a complex event, when eternity broke through into time, when humanity's need, Christ's mission, and all the parallel, inter-related aspects of God's nature came together.

When we preach the gospel, we usually try to explain why Jesus died and what happened on the cross. It is easy, however, to focus on just one aspect or accomplishment of his death, and to present an incomplete or unbalanced picture of salvation. We must work hard to understand and proclaim the full picture of salvation in all its glory.

When we take an overview of the New Testament, we see that Jesus died for several parallel reasons which fulfilled the complementary purposes of his incarnation and messianic mission. Our understanding of 'salvation' needs to incorporate all these simultaneously.

Victory

Jesus died to rescue humanity from the grip of death and Satan. Through his death, he destroyed the one who had the power of death, and released those held captive by their fear of death. He returned to earth in resurrection triumph, and ascended to heaven with 'the keys of hell and death'. We see this in Hebrews 2:14–15 and Revelation 1:18.

Hebrews 2:14–15 ☐
Revelation 1:18 ☐

Jesus died and rose as 'the Victor' who destroys Satan's last weapon, establishes the kingdom of God, sets people free, and fulfils every aspect of the Old Testament reparation sacrifice. This is salvation from Satan so that we can live in Christ's victory and freedom.

Atonement

Jesus also died to make atonement for humanity's sin. On the cross, he appeased God's wrath and delivered us from sin. He did this by accepting the blame, enduring the agony of separation from the Father, taking the faults of many on himself, and winning eternal reconciliation.

By his death, Jesus earnt forgiveness, and fulfilled every aspect of the Old Testament sin sacrifice – and all the prophecies which point to substitutionary death by God's Servant as the only acceptable ground by which God can satisfy himself and cleanse and justify a sinner. This is salvation from sin and God's wrath so that we can have Christ's righteousness and stand before God.

SALVATION AND ATONEMENT

Revelation

In-and-through his sacrificial death, Jesus supremely revealed the full glory of God's holy nature – his goodness, mercy, grace, truth, patience, forgiveness, righteousness, peace, self-control, gentleness, self-effacement, trustfulness, faith, justice and love.

On the cross, God revealed his perfect justice by condemning all sins and bearing his just punishment for evil, and he demonstrated his immeasurable, inexhaustible, unknowable, self-giving love.

At the same time, Jesus also revealed ideal human behaviour in comforting a criminal, asking God to forgive those who tortured him, committing himself into God's hands, and providing for all time an example of perfect submissive obedience. In this way, he fulfilled all the details of the Old Testament wholly-burnt sacrifice.

This is salvation from alienation and isolation so that we can live in fellowship with God.

New life

And Jesus also died in excruciating pain to struggle and strain for the birth of a new creation. After six hellish hours of spiritual childbirth he was, like the panting deer of Psalm 42:1–2, deeply spiritually thirsty. As he died 'in labour' he could cry, 'It's finished; it's completed; I've done it' because, like the Servant in Isaiah 53:10, he had seen his offspring.

Psalm 42:1–2 ☐
Isaiah 53:10 ☐

So Jesus went to the cross to travail and give birth to a new creation which would reproduce the divine nature, and to fulfil every aspect of the Old Testament communion sacrifice. This is salvation from eternal death so that we can live eternally with God's new life.

Full salvation

It is tragic that the whole church has seldom embraced and proclaimed every aspect of salvation, for all are biblical and all are grace.

For example, many congregations concentrate on Jesus' triumph on the cross, and stress his authority over Satan. Others focus on Jesus' atonement, and emphasise his forgiveness of sin. Some concentrate on Jesus' revelation of ideal humanity; and a few stress his manifestation of God's glory.

We do need to appreciate the distinctive emphases of other Christian traditions, and to stand with them in their worship and proclamation. But it is surely better for every congregation to grasp the fullness of salvation, so that we all understand, appropriate, experience and proclaim the full world-changing glory of the cross.

For the rest of this book, we focus in turn on the different aspects of salvation. The rest of this chapter considers salvation in terms of atonement; in Part Six, we think about it in terms of revelation; in Part Seven, in terms of victory; and, in Part Eight, in terms of new life.

ATONEMENT

Most technical theological terms are derived from Latin and Greek roots. 'Atonement' and 'Gospel' are the only important words which come from the Old English, from 'Anglo Saxon'.

As we see in *Reaching the Lost*, the word 'gospel' originally meant 'Good Speak', but it has come to be used in many different ways. It is the same with atonement. Many leaders use the word almost as a synonym for forgiveness, but this is incorrect. Atonement is based in the Old English word 'one', and this was extended to 'onement' to mean what we would call today 'unity'. This means that 'unification' is the closest modern word to the original meaning of 'atonement'.

Some people have suggested that atonement should be pronounced 'at-one-ment' so that the true meaning is made clear. This would be helpful, but the prefix 'at' is not really a preposition; it is merely due to a medieval mix-up of the Old English word 'onement' and the Latin word 'adunamentum' (which means 'towards oneness').

Quite simply, atonement means 'to make at one' and it refers to the complete *process* of bringing those who are estranged into oneness, into unity. Within the whole subject of salvation, the process of atonement includes forgiveness, propitiation, redemption, justification mediation, adoption and reconciliation.

These technical terms develop or illustrate aspects of the atonement process, but they are neither synonyms for atonement nor separate processes.

We have seen that some translations of the Bible render the Hebrew word *kaphar* as 'atone', and that 'cover' is more accurate. The Day of Atonement, however, makes the meaning of atonement quite plain, for it involves the whole process of salvation – a full confession of sin; a substitutionary sacrifice which includes a death for sin and a driving away of sin (the power of sin and the memory of sin); the ministry of a mediator between God and his people; and reconciliation between God and his people evidenced by the high priest's safe entry into the Holy of holies. We see this full process in Leviticus 16:11–15.

Leviticus 16:11–15 ☐

Jesus the atonement

Hebrews 9:1–10:39 reveals that the ritual of the Day of Atonement clearly foreshadowed the atoning work of Christ. For example,

Hebrews 9:1–10:39 ☐

- Jesus is our great high priest, and his sacrificial blood fulfilled the blood of the bulls and goats. Unlike the Old Testament high priests, however, the sinless Christ did not have to make sacrifice for any sins of his own.

- As the high priest entered the Holy of holies with the blood of his sacrificial victim, so Jesus entered heaven to appear before the Father on behalf of his people.

- The high priest had to offer sin sacrifices every year, and this annual repetition reminded the people that perfect atonement had not yet been provided. Jesus, however, through his own blood, eternally reconciled us to the Father.

- The sin offerings could cleanse the sinner only ceremonially and outwardly, they could not cleanse internally. Through his better sacrifice, however, Jesus purged our conscience from dead works.

- The tabernacle was designed to teach Israel that sin hindered access to God's presence. Only the high priest, and he only once a year clutching sacrificial blood, could enter the Holy of holies. Jesus, however, through a 'new and living way' has entered heaven. We no longer need stand away from God; instead, through Christ, we can approach God face-to-face.

- On the Day of Atonement, the flesh of sin was burned outside the camp of Israel. Jesus also suffered outside the gates of Jerusalem to deal with his people's sin and unite them with God.

Word pictures

The New Testament uses some special words to describe four aspects of the atonement process. Many believers think that these are technical words which refer to distinct doctrines; they are, however, just inspired metaphors which the writers use to illustrate parts of the process.

We must understand this, for we can stray into confusion or error if we press a metaphor too far or imagine that it is directly analogous.

1. *propitiation*

Romans 3:24–25; 1 John 2:1–2 and 4:10 use the Greek word *hilasmos* as a metaphor for Christ's work, and this is usually translated as 'propitiation'. This word-picture was taken from Greek religious life, and it describes the process by which their pagan gods were appeased or placated, and good will was earnt.

Propitiation is clearly not an analogy because neither Testament presents God as an angry deity whose affections need to be bought or who can be bribed into changing his mind.

Instead, propitiation is a metaphor which points to God's just wrath against sin and to God's provision of the substitute who willingly 'completed' or 'exhausted' or 'satisfied' God's wrath.

In Greek life, the people had to appease their angry gods with gifts for the gods did nothing. In his grace, however, the living God willed, initiated, provided and accomplished everything for us so that he could act self-consistently and be both loving and just at the same time.

Leviticus 17:11; Romans 3:25 and 1 John 4:10 underline the grace of God in the propitiatory aspect of the atoning process. As a result, we can say that God in his holy wrath needed to be propitiated, that God in his holy love initiated the necessary propitiating, and that God-in-Christ died as the propitiation for our sins.

2. *redemption*

The word-picture *apolutrosis* was taken from Greek business life, where it described the process by which objects or property were purchased for a fixed price: it was also commonly used to describe the purchase and/or release of slaves and the 'ransom' of prisoners-of-war.

The idea of redemption is used extensively in the Old Testament to describe the purchase of property, animals, persons and the Jewish nation. We see this, for example, in Exodus 13:13; 30:12–16; 34:20; Leviticus 25:25–28; 27; Numbers 3:40–51; 18:14–17; Ruth 3–4; 2 Samuel 7:23; Isaiah 43:1–4; Jeremiah 32:6–8.

In the Old Testament, the payment of a price is always the essence of redemption by humans. Where God, however, is described as the redeemer, the price always refers to the costly effort he makes: we see this in Exodus 6:6; Deuteronomy 9:26; Nehemiah 1:10 and Psalm 77:15.

In the New Testament, 'redemption' is a metaphor which points to the *plight* from which we are redeemed; the *price* with which we are redeemed; and the *proprietary rights* of the redeemer.

Passages like Galatians 3:13; 4:5; Ephesians 1:7; Colossians 1:13–14; Titus 2:14; Hebrews 9:15 and 1 Peter 1:18 describe *the plight* from which humanity has been redeemed. Christ gave himself to redeem us from *all* the consequences of the Fall. We have been able to experience his redemption since Calvary, but we are still waiting for the ultimate 'day of redemption' when we will be made perfect and all creation will be liberated from its bondage to decay. Until then, the Holy Spirit is the guarantee and first-fruit of our final redemption. We see this in Luke 21:28; Ephesians 1:14; 4:30 and Romans 8:18–23.

The New Testament makes it plain that Christ himself, and particularly his blood, was *the price* paid (but the Bible never presses the metaphor too far and enquires to whom the price was paid). We see the price in Mark 10:45; Romans 3:24–25; Galatians 3:13; 4:4–5; Ephesians 1:7; 1 Timothy 2:5–6; Titus 2:14; 1 Peter 1:18–19.

The Scriptures also use the redemption image to stress that the redeemer has *proprietary rights* over his purchase. Jesus' lordship over both the church and individual Christians is attributed to his having bought us with his own blood. We see this, for example, in Acts 20:28; 1 Corinthians 6:18–20; 7:23; 2 Peter 2:1; Revelation 1:5–6; 5:9; 14:3–4.

3. *justification*

The third illustration was drawn from Greek law courts, where *dikaioo*, justification, was the precise opposite of condemnation. Greek and Roman judges pronounced the accused either 'guilty' or 'not guilty', they were either 'justified' or 'condemned', and Paul uses this as a metaphor in Romans 5:18 and 8:34.

The term 'justification' illustrates God's action in declaring sinners free of blame on the basis of the substitution of his Son who exhausts the sinners' judgement and 'imputes' his righteousness to them so that they can stand before God with Christ's righteousness.

'Justification' is simply a first-century illustration of God's official declaration of righteousness on the basis of his objective legal pardon. It is a word-picture about a change in legal status – it sheds no light on, and makes no reference to, a change of nature. God does, of course, change human nature through regeneration and sanctification, but the image of justification does not point to these aspects of salvation.

Paul develops this metaphor and shows that we are justified:

- *by God's grace alone*; it is entirely his initiative and his accomplishment – Romans 3:10, 20, 24; 8:33
- *by Christ's blood alone*; it is a precise act of justice – Romans 5:9

  When God justifies sinners, he is not declaring bad people good, or saying that they are not sinners; instead, he is pronouncing them legally righteous, officially not guilty, because he-in-Christ has borne the penalty of their law-breaking.

- *through faith alone*; we must receive what his grace offers and depend entirely on what God has done for us in Christ – Romans 3:28; 5:1; Galatians 2:16; Philippians 3:9.

  The old Reformation formula helpfully summarises the biblical teaching on justification as 'by grace alone, through Christ alone, by faith alone'.

- *together in Christ*; it is also corporate, without any ethnic, national or gender barriers – Galatians 2:17; 3:26–29; Romans 8:1; 2 Corinthians 5:21; Ephesians 1:6

4.   *reconciliation*

The fourth metaphor, reconciliation, *katallasso*, is taken from everyday Greek life, where it was used to describe the healing of an estrangement between two parties. It referred to old friends or relatives making up after an argument or quarrel.

This picture points to the great purpose of the atonement, to the divine yearning behind the whole of salvation. We are forgiven, God is propitiated, we are redeemed and justified, we are delivered from Satan, God reveals himself and reproduces his nature *so that* God can reconcile us with him and we can live with him in the eternal relationship of perfect fellowship that he intended in Eden.

It is important we recognise, however, that this picture is always used of us being reconciled to God, and never of God being reconciled to God. God needs to be propitiated, not reconciled; and we need to be reconciled, not propitiated!

This relationship is so important, so fundamental, that one metaphor will not do. The Bible also uses the metaphors of 'adoption' into God's family, 'peace' with God and 'access' to God as it struggles to describe this indescribable cross-made relationship.

We see these metaphors in, for example, John 1:12–13; 1 John 3:1–10; Romans 5:1–2; 8:14–17; Galatians 3:26–29; 4:1–7; Ephesians 2:17–18; 3:12; Hebrews 10:19–22 and 1 Peter 3:18.

Reconciliation is a word-picture for the relationship with God which is both the purpose and the fruit of salvation. But it is only when we have been forgiven, redeemed and justified that we have the peaceable access to God as his adopted children which is reconciliation.

But biblical reconciliation is not only about a renewed relationship with God, it is also about a new relationship with other people in-and-through Christ – Ephesians 2:11–22 concentrates on this aspect of reconciliation. And it is also about the cosmic reconciliation referred to in Colossians 1:15–20 – this is the 'world' dynamic of salvation which we stress in *Knowing the Father* and *Reaching the Lost*.

2 Corinthians 5:18–21 reveals much about reconciliation. It underlines that:

- *God is the great all-grace author or initiator of reconciliation* – he willed it, he began it
- *Christ is the agent of reconciliation* – God has done it all in-and-through his Son
- *we are the ambassadors of reconciliation* – we must appropriate it, live it, preach it and practise it

John 1:12–13 ☐
1 John 3:1–10 ☐
Romans 5:1–2 ☐
8:14–17 ☐
Galatians
3:26–29 ☐
4:1–7 ☐
Ephesians
2:17–18 ☐
3:12 ☐
Hebrews
10:19–22 ☐
1 Peter 3:18 ☐
Ephesians
2:11–22 ☐
Colossians
1:15–20 ☐
2 Corinthians
5:18–21 ☐

Atonement

These four word-pictures from first-century life are simply 'colloquial' illustrations of overlapping aspects of the atonement. They cannot be fitted together into a neat theory of atonement; they merely provide us with insights into a mystery, not a complete doctrine.

Nevertheless, each metaphors emphasises three basic principles of the atonement, of God's process of unification:

- *humanity has a very great need* – propitiation points to God's wrath against our sin, redemption to our slavery to sin, justification to our guilt before God, and reconciliation to our alienation from God

- *God is all-grace* – it is he who in his love has taken the initiative and propitiated his own wrath, paid the price to redeem us from slavery, endured his own punishment to declare us righteous, and reconciled us to himself

- *it has been accomplished only through the substitutionary sacrifice of Christ's blood* – we see this in Romans 3:25; 5:9; Ephesians 1:7; 2:23 and Colossians 1:20

The death of Jesus on the cross as the substitute was the once-and-for-all single sacrifice of atonement because of which God averted his wrath from us, *and* it was the ransom price by which we have been redeemed, *and* it was the condemnation of the innocent by which the guilty might be justified – *so that* we can be one with God, one with each other, and one with creation for all eternity.

This is the sheer greatness of just a single aspect of our salvation – there are three more complementary aspects still to consider.

Sidebar references:
Romans 3:25 ☐
5:9 ☐
Ephesians 1:7 ☐
2:23 ☐
Colossians 1:20 ☐

PART SIX

salvation and revelation

Throughout this *Sword of the Spirit* series, we emphasise that God's words and God's works are all essentially self-revelatory. Because God is, by definition, utterly self-consistent, all his deeds, words, thoughts and attitudes must conform both to each other and to the totality of his holy character.

This means that God's supreme act of salvation *for* the world on the cross must also be God's supreme act of self-revelation *to* the world through the death of his beloved Son.

THE GLORY OF GOD

In *Glory in the Church*, we see that *kabod* is the Hebrew word for glory. The Old Testament occasionally uses *kabod* to describe a particular person's material prosperity, physical splendour or good reputation, but it is generally reserved for God himself.

The Old Testament uses the expression 'the glory of God' in two different ways: first, as a parallel term to 'the Name of God' which refers to the self-revealed character of God; and, second, as a *visible* revelation of God's localised presence. Put simply, God's *kabod* shows people *where he is* and *what he is like*: it is a localised, visible manifestation of his absolute holiness.

In the Old Testament, God's glory was revealed:

- *in the created world* – Psalm 19:1; 29:9; Isaiah 6:3 (and Matthew 6:29) report that heaven and earth were filled with God's glory

- *to the redeemed people of God* – Numbers 14:22; Psalm 97:2–6; Isaiah 35:2; 40:5 and Exodus 33:18 – 34:7 describe how God showed his glory in delivering Israel from Egypt and Babylon

- *at the hour of sacrifice* – Exodus 24; Leviticus 9:6–24; 1 Kings 8:1–11 describe how God showed his glory in response to his people's grateful sacrifices

The Greek word for glory is *doxa*, and this is normally used in the New Testament to describe Jesus' revelation, by grace and powerful deeds, of God's presence and nature. The glory of God seen in Jesus demonstrates that God is present in person, *and* it reveals the full extent of his regal authority and humble, self-sacrificing nature.

Hebrews 1:3 shows that Jesus was always the outshining of God's glory; but his death on the cross was the supreme moment (this side of the Second Coming) of the revelation of God's glory. We see this, for example, in John 7:39; 12:23–28; 13:31; 17:5 and Hebrews 2:9.

Luke 9:32; John 2:1–11 and 11:1–44 show that God's glory (his local presence and nature) were displayed at the Cana wedding, the Bethany cemetery and the Transfiguration; but his glory (his local presence and nature) was most apparent at Calvary – for there was seen the complete self-revelation of God's nature, the greatest possible demonstration of his grace and love, the supreme manifestation of his absolute holiness, and a perfect display of his presence, power and self-sacrificing nature.

Quite simply, the cross was the most visible revelation, so far, of God's localised presence in the world and of God's holy nature to the world: it was the quintessence of glory.

The idea of 'God's glory seen in Christ Jesus' (his localised presence and personal nature revealed through Jesus) is particularly strong in

John's gospel. It shows that God's presence and nature are manifested in Jesus' miracles, which it calls 'signs'; but it also stresses that God's glory is seen in Jesus' willing weakness, in the voluntary self-sacrifice of his incarnation – we see this, for example, in John 1:14.

Tabernacle glory

John 1:14 contains an important allusion to the Old Testament. The Greek word *eskenosen* is translated in some versions simply as 'dwelt', but it literally means 'pitched a tent' and is a direct reference to the Old Testament Tabernacle.

John 1:14 shows that, even though the Word has become human flesh, he has not ceased to be holy God. Instead, God has 'tented' or 'tabernacled' in human flesh so that he can live for a while among his people. This means that the incarnation is the fulfilment of the Exodus 25:8–9 foreshadowing – when Israel was told to make a tent or sanctuary (the Tabernacle) so that God could dwell among his people.

The Tabernacle, and later the Temple, was the site of God's localised presence on earth, and Ezekiel 43:7; Joel 3:17 and Zechariah 2:10 looked forward to the day when God would again 'pitch his tent' in Zion. John 1:14 implicitly claims that the incarnate Jesus is the fulfilment of this prophetic promise.

God's glory was associated with the Tabernacle and Temple – we see this in Exodus 24:9–25:9; 40:34; 1 Kings 8:10–11; Ezekiel 11:23 and 44:4. It is a natural progression, therefore, for John 1:14 to present Jesus as the new tabernacle who is constantly (rather than occasionally) filled with the glory of God, with God's personal presence and nature.

(It is interesting to note Mark 9:2–8 which records the disciples' assumption that they should construct a tent or tabernacle because they had seen God's glory.)

We know that glory reveals God's *presence* and his *nature*. So, just as Exodus 34:5–8 reports that God showed his visible presence and revealed himself as merciful, gracious and abounding in truth, John 1:14 comments that the glory of God seen in Jesus is full of grace and truth.

Tabernacle glory was closely linked to sacrifice. In the Old Testament, God's glory was often revealed at times of sacrifice – for

John 1:14 ☐

Exodus 25:8–9 ☐

Ezekiel 43:7 ☐
Joel 3:17 ☐
Zechariah 2:10 ☐

Exodus 24:9–25:9 ☐
40:34 ☐
1 Kings 8:10–11 ☐
Ezekiel 11:23 ☐
44:4 ☐

Exodus 34:5–8 ☐

example, Exodus 24; 40:9–35; Leviticus 9:6–24 and 1 Kings 8:1–11. So, in the New Testament, his glory is associated with the Son's self-sacrificial, 'tabernacle' incarnation which culminated in his death as the once-and-for-all substitute sacrifice.

All the Gospels anticipate a revelation of glory through the cross, but they look forward to it in slightly different ways. In Luke 24:26, for example, the suffering of the cross is the pathway to future glory, while John 12:20–28; 13:30–32 and 17:1 show that the cross is the actual time and place of glorification.

It is important to recognise that John 12:20–28; 13:30–32 and 17:1 describe the glorification of the cross in terms of the Father *and* the Son together. The presence and nature of God the Father and God the Son are both revealed by the cross; perfect divinity and perfect humanity are both displayed in the drama of Calvary.

On a simple wooden gibbet, the holy goodness of God and the best possible example of human goodness were set before the whole world – and we must gaze on them together as they reveal God's holy nature and remind us of what we should be.

DIVINE JUSTICE AND LOVE

Romans 3:25–26 and 5:8 declare that Christ's death was a public demonstration of both God's justice and his love. We have already noted that God's self-consistency was one of the driving factors behind the cross, now we see that God not only 'satisfied' his justice and love on the cross, he also revealed them to the whole world.

God's justice

Until the cross, God's justice had not been startlingly obvious on earth. Many sinners had prospered, much evil had gone unpunished, and God had often appeared to be impotent, unjust and morally indifferent.

In passages like Genesis 18:25, and throughout Job, Proverbs and Ecclesiastes, the Bible records how the characters and authors of the Scriptures struggled with this dilemma. They wanted to know why the wicked flourished and the innocent suffered, why sinners went unpunished while the righteous were struck by disasters, why God did not always protect his people, answer their prayers, and reward their righteousness.

The Old Testament handles this by looking forward to the final judgement, by proclaiming that though sinners may prosper for a while they will face the righteous judgement of God. We see this, for example, in a passage like Psalm 73.

Psalm 73 ☐

The New Testament repeats this promise of a future, final judgement in, for example, Acts 17:30–31; Romans 2:3 and 2 Peter 3:3–9; but it also looks backwards to the judgement of the cross.

Acts 17:30–31 ☐
Romans 2:3 ☐
2 Peter 3:3–9 ☐

Romans 3:21–26; Hebrews 9:15 and 10:4 declare that the decisive judgement of God has already taken place, and they stress that God's Old Testament inaction had been merely a gracious postponement of judgement rather than an unjust cancellation.

Romans 3:21–26 ☐
Hebrews 9:15 ☐
10:4 ☐

At the cross, by his sacrifice, God finally and fully revealed his perfect justice by condemning all sins in Christ; and, on the cross, he gave a visible proof of his innate justice by himself bearing, in Christ, his just punishment for all the evil in the world.

Since his sacrifice on the cross, God can no longer be accused of condoning evil or of being unjust, because his justice in judging and punishing sin has, once-and-for-all, been clearly and convincingly revealed to all creation.

God's love

It is much the same with God's love; until the cross, it had also not been especially apparent to humanity. Disease, disasters, decay, even death, all argued against God being characterised by love. Tragedy, torture, tyranny and tribulation all seemed irreconcilable with a God of love. But, at the cross, God finally revealed to humanity the extent of his immeasurable, inexhaustible, unknowable, self-giving love.

The New Testament always defines love in terms of God's sacrifice on the cross – we see this particularly clearly in Romans 5:8; 1 John 3:16; 4:7–21.

Romans 5:8 ☐
1 John 3:16 ☐
4:7–21 ☐

All humanity experiences something of love in this life, but the Bible claims that only one act of pure, selfless love, untainted by any ulterior motive, has ever been performed – the self-giving of God in Christ on the cross for undeserving sinners.

Romans 5:8 suggests that God's revelation of his love on the cross had three distinct aspects:

- he gave *his Son* – John 3:16; Romans 8:32;
- he gave his Son *to die* – Philippians 2:7–8
- he gave his Son to die *for us* – for his sinful, ungodly, powerless enemies – Romans 3:18, 23; 5:6, 10; 8:7

At the cross, stretched by soldiers between two thieves, the Son died – and the Father left him alone. Why? Because of their love for the thieves, the torturers, and all those who pleaded for the Son's death.

At the cross, God gave everything because of his love for those who deserve nothing. The Father gave the Son for those who prefer to worship other gods, and the Son gave himself for those who steadfastly ignore him. They both surrendered their relationship with each other because of their unimaginable love for the whole world and every member of humanity.

Since the dreadful agony and divine separation of the sacrifice at Calvary, nobody can look at a cross and question God's love, because nothing could demonstrate God's love more clearly than this totally selfless self-sacrifice.

The sacrificial death of Jesus took place because of God's justice and God's love: there was no other motivation. As we have seen, Jesus' death had many consequences, but among them was this revelation of God's perfect love and justice *and* also of the perfect human example for all people to imitate.

It follows, therefore, that those who walk in Jesus' footsteps should ensure that all their sacrifices are similarly motivated by God's absolute justice and his unlimited selfless love – without holding anything back, without any subtle attempts at manipulation, and without any sense of self-sufficient detachment.

When this is so, we can be confident of two things: first, that our sacrifices will reveal something of God's glory, of his character and local presence, to the people around us in a way that nothing else can; and, second, that the God of self-sacrifice will share deeply in our willing agony, isolation and deprivation.

DIVINE WISDOM AND POWER

The first eleven chapters of Romans are Paul's classic exposition of the gospel. In them, he describes how God presented Christ as a substitute sacrifice, justifies us through faith in Christ, starts to transform us by the work of the Spirit, and is shaping us into a new community into which all people are admitted on the same terms as Jews.

Before Paul moves on to apply the gospel in Romans 12–16, he pauses for a moment's reflection. In Romans 11:33–36, he praises the ingenious wisdom which devised salvation in such a way that it simultaneously meets all the needs of both humanity and God's self-consistent nature. We have seen that the early chapters of Romans stress the revelation on the cross of God's perfect justice and love, 11:33–36 now shows that the cross also reveals God's perfect wisdom.

Romans
11:33–36 ☐

The opposite of human wisdom

Paul repeats this idea in 1 Corinthians 1:17–2:5. He stresses here both that the cross reveals God's wisdom and power, and that this is the opposite of the world's wisdom and power.

1 Corinthians
1:17–2:5 ☐

In 1 Corinthians 1:22, Paul shows that the Jews and the Greeks were laying down different conditions for accepting the gospel: the Jews were demanding powerful signs and the Greeks were looking for great wisdom. The two groups of people wanted the gospel message to prove its authenticity to them by inherent power and wisdom.

1 Corinthians 1:23 shows, however, that Paul's message neither impressed them nor met their demands. The cross offended them both equally; to them, it was 'foolishness' and a 'stumbling block'.

But, for Paul, the cross was the exact opposite. In 1:24 he reveals that the crucified-in-weakness Christ is actually God's power, and that the apparently-foolish Christ is himself the wisdom of God. Then, in 1:25, Paul makes it plain that God's foolishness is greater than human wisdom, and that his weakness is stronger than human strength.

This means that though the cross appears to most people to be the height of impotence and folly, it is actually the supreme manifestation of God's personal wisdom and power.

Paul explains this in 1 Corinthians 1:26–31 in terms of the Corinthians' experience. Most of Paul's readers were not wise or influential people; in fact, God had deliberately selected the foolish and feeble to shame the wise and strong, and to exclude any possibility of human boasting. This would have been entirely inappropriate because it was entirely God himself who had united them to Christ, and it was Christ who had become their wisdom and power.

In 1 Corinthians 1:30–31, Paul underlines the multi-faceted nature of salvation by summarising the message of the cross as a grace-gift of four great blessings in Christ: God's personal wisdom, righteousness, sanctification and redemption.

God's personal wisdom

Paul's suggestion that Jesus is God's wisdom present in person resonates with Old Testament significance. The books of Job, Psalms, Proverbs, Ecclesiastes and Song of Songs are 'the Wisdom literature', and Proverbs 1–9 contains the clearest and most detailed biblical description of God's wisdom.

These important chapters personify 'Wisdom', contrast her with folly (the refusal to know or acknowledge God), and contain a remarkable series of claims and promises which are all fulfilled and repeated by Jesus (the 'Word') in John's Gospel – for example, Proverbs 7:2; 8:6–8, 17, 18–21, 32–35 and 9:5–6.

Then, in 1 Corinthians 2:1–5, Paul illustrates God's wisdom and power from his personal experience. He reports that he had not visited Corinth in his own strength or with a message of human wisdom. Instead, he had brought the apparently foolish message of the cross, and he had gone in weakness, fear and trembling – relying on the Holy Spirit to confirm his words and convince people of their truth.

Paul's purpose in going to the Corinthians in folly and feebleness was to ensure that people's faith rested firmly on God's personal power and wisdom rather than human ideas and abilities. This is a key principle of evangelism which we need continually to absorb and to apply.

The message of the cross will never be humanly popular because God has chosen to reveal his wisdom and power through human foolishness and weakness. But 1 Corinthians 1:24 shows that the crucified Christ is God's wisdom and 1:30 declares that he is ours too.

THE GLORY OF GOD

The cross reveals God's great wisdom in managing to save sinners and satisfy his love and justice; and Romans 1:16 declares that the cross is also the revelation of God's power for the salvation of all who believe.

Romans 1:16

This means that we can see God's justice, love, wisdom and power when we look carefully at the cross. It is easy to emphasise one aspect of God's character more than another. We can be so taken by God's justice in dealing with our sin that we neglect the love which bore the judgement in our place. And we can be so thrilled by the power which saves us that we overlook the wisdom which devised our salvation.

But it is all God in person, and not a collection of depersonalised attributes. Rather than trying to compare the different aspects of God's divine nature, we should rejoice that – through the saving cross – he has revealed the full extent of his holy nature so clearly and completely.

PERFECT HUMAN GOODNESS

The cross was not only the supreme revelation of God's glory, it was also the perfect example of human goodness. The Father sent the Son as the 'fully-God, fully-human being' not only to reveal his divine self, but also to show humanity the ideal way to live and die.

Before the creation of time, space and matter, Jesus was with God and he was God. He was all-powerful, all-seeing, all-knowing, all-loving and all-present. He dwelt in perpetual glory and was all-glorious, and this *visible* glory was Jesus' first sacrifice.

Philippians 2:5–8 shows that the Father did not make the Son surrender his *visible* glory; he relinquished it willingly. Jesus' state was divine, yet he did not 'cling to' (or 'grasp after' – the Greek is ambiguous) his equality with God. Instead, he emptied himself by shedding every attribute which visibly expressed God's nature.

Philippians 2:5–8

Jesus laid aside his visible majesty and 'tabernacled' himself in human flesh. He put down his omnipotence, omnipresence and omniscience, and 'pitched his tent' in all the human weaknesses except sin.

He stepped out of the visible glory to which he was entitled and stopped looking like God. Of course, Jesus did not cease to be God because he did not give up his divine nature; instead, he sacrificed the public treatment and honour due to him as God, and then he assumed the condition of a human slave and made himself as nothing in human eyes.

Willing self-denial

This self-denial was seen in Jesus' willing acceptance of life as a vulnerable foetus in a female womb, as a helpless babe in Bethlehem, as a powerless refugee in Egypt, as an illegitimate child in Nazareth, as a humble carpenter in Galilee, as a homeless wanderer throughout Israel, as a convicted criminal at Calvary, and so on.

This was the self-denying, self-effacing way of living that Jesus freely chose, for he deliberately sacrificed his visible glory to embrace the supposedly lowest levels of humanity. And he calls us to follow him.

Because Jesus was fully God, he could have arranged things differently. He could have 'pitched his tent' in an emperor's palace; he could have continued to radiate the visible glory of God; he could even have resuscitated his earthly father when he died. But, by a deliberate act of self-denial, Jesus chose to personify perfect human contentment with obscurity, powerlessness, indifference and apparent insignificance.

When John the Baptist called people to repent and to evidence this by being baptised, Jesus joined the queue of sinners. He did not ask John to stand aside and let him take over; instead, he stood where sinners stood. Matthew 3:15 records that, when John protested, Jesus insisted that this was the right way to act.

Willing self-denial dominated Jesus' human life and ministry. He spent six weeks in the wilderness without food and resisted unparalleled temptations. He ministered without expecting any gratitude or earthly reward. He entrusted his money to a man who misappropriated it. He embraced lepers and befriended social outcasts. He washed feet and was repeatedly misunderstood and misrepresented.

As we have seen, Jesus was undoubtedly Isaiah's suffering servant – but few people recognised this. Pilate realised that Jesus was the real king of the Jews; a few disciples guessed that he was the Son of the living God; and most people probably thought that he was a very good man. But Jesus was not the kind of human king or perfect person that people expected or wanted.

They longed for the ideal Man promised in Daniel 7:13–14, who would be served by people of all nations. Jesus was that 'Son of Man', but he had come to serve and not to be served, to ask us to serve others with him rather than just to serve him with others.

The perfect example of humanity demonstrated by Jesus (God's ideal way for all people to live) is characterised by selfless, self-giving, self-sacrificing, self-denial. This reaches its fulfilment, and is revealed most clearly and completely, on the cross. It should be obvious that Jesus' willing acceptance of the cross is the natural conclusion of the way that he lived as a human.

Willing self-sacrifice

As soon as the disciples realised that Jesus was the *Christos*, the 'Anointed Man' or *Messiah*, he explained what this meant – in Matthew 16:21; Mark 8:31–32; Luke 9:22.

This was anathema to the disciples, so Peter took Jesus aside to remonstrate. He neither understood nor believed that God's ideal way could involve suffering, rejection and death. But Jesus rebuked him, and then told the disciples, in Matthew 16:24; Mark 8:34 and Luke 9:23, that the divine demand for self-sacrifice applied to them too.

As the time of Jesus' ultimate sacrifice drew near, Jesus taught his disciples more clearly about human self-sacrifice. For example:

- *he taught them the secret of human greatness* – Matthew 20:25–27; Mark 10:41–45; Luke 22:24–27

- *he demonstrated the unpretentious peaceful nature of his rule* – Matthew 21:1–11; Mark 11:1–11; Luke 19:28–38; John 12:12–16

- *he commended the widow's discreet sacrifice* – Mark 12:41–44

- *he applauded Mary's extravagant giving* – Matthew 26:6–13; Mark 14:3–9; John 12:1–16

- *he revealed the perfection of his love and instructed his disciples to follow his example* – John 13:1–16

Most important of all, Jesus taught his disciples the vital spiritual principle that willing self-sacrifice is the secret of fruitfulness. This is written deep across God's creation: before any seed can multiply it must die and cease to be. If the seed seeks to preserve its own independent existence, it remains a single grain; but it yields a rich harvest when it dies and disappears.

Jesus took this principle and applied it to himself in John 12:23–33. But he was not thinking only of himself for, in verses 25–26, he expressly applied the same principle to all who would follow him.

The man on the cross

Jesus' death on the cross not only revealed the full nature of God, it also provided a perfect example of God's ideal pattern for humanity.

While he suffered, Jesus made time to demonstrate perfect human behaviour by asking God to forgive those who had tortured him, and by comforting a criminal with the promise that he would be with him in paradise. And, when he died, Jesus left everything behind, provided for his mother, and committed his spirit into God's hands.

Luke always draws his readers' attention to the fully-human side of Jesus. His account of the cross is shorter than the others, yet somehow conveys a remarkable intensity of anguish. Luke 22:42–44 shows Jesus enduring unparalleled spiritual agony as he wrestles with God's will: it is the most telling New Testament insight into the humanity of the perfect Son of Man.

In the different reports of the crucifixion, it is only Luke who notes that Jesus died committing his spirit into the hands of the Father, and that Jesus continued his ministry of forgiveness right to the very end.

Luke leaves it to the other Gospel writers to reveal that Jesus' death is 'a ransom for many' and a victory over Satan. He concentrates on revealing that Jesus' death on the cross is the ultimate example of perfect human goodness.

For Luke, the cross is where the Messiah, the 'anointed man', fulfils his Isaiah 53 destiny by accepting and enduring rejection, suffering and death. This is the Christ who calls his disciples to follow him, to follow his example, to take up their crosses (every day, according to Luke) and to share his ideal way of living and dying.

PART SEVEN

salvation and victory

The New Testament echoes with the early church's cries of victory. Passages like Romans 8:37; 1 Corinthians 15:57; 2 Corinthians 2:14 and Revelation 2–3 illustrate the early believer's conviction that they were victorious conquerors, triumphant winners, glorious overcomers.

They knew, however, that they owed their victory completely to the victorious Jesus. Colossians 2:15; Revelation 3:21; 5:5 and 12:11 show that it is Christ who overcame and triumphed – and that he did so on the cross.

We can be so familiar with the idea of 'victory on-and-through the cross' that we forget how absurd it appears to most unbelievers. How can a crucified Christ be a conqueror? How can a victim be a victor? How can an executed criminal, who was rejected, betrayed, denied and deserted by his own disciples, be deemed triumphant?

Most people think that it makes more sense to describe the cross as a place of death and defeat; yet Christians claim that the ultimate truth is the opposite of the human appearance. It may seem that evil triumphed over goodness at the cross, but the Bible declares that it was the place where goodness conquered evil. It may seem that Christ

Romans 8:37 ☐

1 Corinthians 15:57 ☐

2 Corinthians 2:14 ☐

Revelation 2–3 ☐

Colossians 2:15 ☐

Revelation 3:21 ☐
5:5 ☐
12:11 ☐

was crushed by earthly powers on the cross, but the Scriptures insist that it was the place where the Seed of the woman finally crushed the serpent's head.

As we have seen, the enigma of Christ's victory is not the full truth of salvation – but it is an important element. The cross is the place of atonement, revelation, reproduction and victory; and our understanding of salvation is imperfect if we neglect any of these aspects of Christ's achievement.

More importantly, our personal experience of salvation is greatly impoverished when we overlook any feature of Calvary. We must not only understand and celebrate the different aspects of salvation, we must also appropriate them all by faith and enter into them fully.

THE PROGRESSIVE VICTORY

Although the Bible declares that Jesus triumphed *decisively* over the devil, and disarmed him completely, at the cross, it also presents a progressive picture of victory which leads towards the decisive moment on the cross and also leads on to its final completion.

Predictions of victory

Genesis 3:15 is usually considered to be the first glimpse of the gospel, the first foreshadowing of the cross, and it points specifically to this 'victory' aspect of salvation.

This first prediction of triumph identified the woman's seed, or offspring, as the one who would be completely victorious. It was later revealed to the prophets that this 'seed' would be the *Messiah*, the *Christos* or 'Anointed Man', who would establish God's righteous rule and eradicate evil.

When we take an overview of the Old Testament, and interpret each passage in the light of the cross, we can see that verses like 1 Chronicles 29:11 (which declare God's then *present* righteous rule in Israel) and Isaiah 9:6–7 (which announce his *future* rule through the Messiah) are further implicit predictions of the Seed's ultimate triumph over the serpent.

SALVATION AND VICTORY

Foretastes of victory

We have seen in *The Rule of God* that the righteous kingdom arrived in-and-with Jesus. If Christ's decisive victory over Satan was achieved in his death on the cross, the early rounds were won in his perfect submission to God throughout his earthly life and in the mighty works which demonstrated his unique anointing and authority.

As soon as Jesus was born, Satan recognised him as his future conqueror and started to attempt to defeat him. For example, he attacked Jesus through:

- *Herod's slaughter of the Bethlehem children* – Matthew 2:1–18
- *the wilderness temptations to avoid the cross* – Matthew 4:1–11
- *the Nazareth congregation's attempts on his life* – Luke 4:28–29
- *the crowds desire to make him a political ruler* – John 6:15
- *Peter's opposition to the way of the cross* – Matthew 16:21–23
- *Judas' betrayal* – Luke 22:1–6; John 13:27

But Jesus was determined to fulfil what had been foretold. He announced that God's kingdom had come to that generation through him, and that his mighty works were the visible proof of its coming.

Through the Gospels, we see God's kingdom advancing and Satan's retreating as demons were cast out, diseases were healed and nature was calmed – for example, Mark 1:24; Matthew 4:23 and Mark 4:39.

Luke 9:1–6 and 10:1–24 describe how Jesus sent twelve apostles and seventy disciples to announce the kingdom's arrival by preaching and healing as his representatives. When they returned, Jesus told them that he had seen Satan fall from heaven as a result of their activities.

Mark 3:27 and Luke 11:21–22 seem to summarise Jesus' understanding of his pre-Calvary struggles with Satan. The devil may have been a very strong man, but a stronger man had come – and he would bind and overpower the strong man and plunder his house.

This binding and overpowering did not take place, however, until the cross. In John 12:31; 14:30 and 16:11, Jesus anticipated the devil's last offensive on the cross, and promised that he would be driven out and condemned. And Hebrews 2:14–15 states that it was *by his death* that Jesus destroyed the devil and liberated his captives.

Matthew 2:1–18 ☐
4:1–11 ☐
Luke 4:28–29 ☐
John 6:15 ☐
Matthew 16:21–23 ☐
Luke 22:1–6 ☐
John 13:27 ☐

Mark 1:24 ☐
Matthew 4:23 ☐
Mark 4:39 ☐

Luke 9:1–6 ☐
10:1–24 ☐

Mark 3:27 ☐
Luke 11:21–22 ☐

John 12:31 ☐
14:30 ☐
16:11 ☐
Hebrews 2:14–15 ☐

The moment of victory

Colossians 2:13–15 is the clearest New Testament statement about the victory of Christ on the cross. In this important passage, the apostle Paul draws together two aspects of salvation.

First, he illustrates God's gracious act of forgiveness on the cross by comparing it to the way that debts were cancelled. Paul shows that God has released us from our moral and spiritual bankruptcy by paying our debts on the cross; and, moreover, that God has also destroyed all the records of our indebtedness.

Paul then describes God's powerful act of conquest on the cross, and shows that he had stripped his opponents of their weapons and exhibited them as impotent, defeated enemies.

We must recognise that Paul uses some vivid physical images to describe an invisible spiritual reality. Just as God did not literally nail a list of our debts on the cross, so Jesus did not literally exhibit defeated demons in Jerusalem.

The deep truth beneath Paul's imagery is that forgiveness and victory both occurred simultaneously and are always inescapably linked. In fact, we can *almost* say that Christ triumphed over evil by repaying our debts, that by delivering us from our sins he delivered us from sin.

We see in *Knowing the Son* that perfect submission is the essence of Jesus' sonship. Just as Jesus overcame the devil during his ministry by resisting all his temptations, and by his perfect submission and obedience to the Father, so he triumphed over the devil on the cross by the perfect obedience described in Romans 5:19 and Philippians 2:8.

The Son's perfect submission was indispensable to salvation. If Jesus had disobeyed for a moment, had deviated one inch from God's path, the devil would have gained a fingerhold and frustrated salvation. But Jesus obeyed the Father completely – and so the devil was routed.

On the cross, the devil provoked Jesus through torture, injustice, lies and insults, but Jesus refused to retaliate. He could have summoned an angelic army to help him, he could have stepped down from the cross; but, instead of overcoming evil with power, he conquered it with good – as Romans 12:21 explains.

The devil used every weapon in his arsenal to tempt Jesus to disobey God, to hate his enemies, to imitate the world's use of power;

SALVATION AND VICTORY

but, by his obedience, self-denial, love and humility, Jesus won the decisive moral victory over evil. In the height of the conflict, he remained uncontaminated and uncompromised by evil.

Despite everything that the devil did at the cross, he could gain no hold on Jesus; and, when Jesus died without sin, the devil had to concede defeat. This means that the long-predicted victory of the Seed, which began during Christ's earthly life and ministry, was decisively accomplished by his death at the cross.

The confirmation of victory

Some believers seem to think that the cross was a temporary defeat and that the resurrection was the real moment of victory. But the cross was the victory and the resurrection was merely the visible proof and public vindication of the victory on the cross. We see this, for example, in Acts 2:24; Ephesians 1:20–23 and 1 Peter 3:22.

Of course, the New Testament always links the cross and the empty tomb together – as in, Mark 8:31; 9:31; 10:34; Luke 24:30–35; John 10:17–18; Acts 2:23–24; Romans 6:1–4; 1 Corinthians 15:1–8; 2 Corinthians 5:15; 1 Thessalonians 4:14 and Revelation 1:18. This means that we should not proclaim the cross without the resurrection or the resurrection without the cross, for Jesus is both the *living Lord* and the *atoning Saviour*.

Despite this unbreakable link, we will understand salvation correctly only when we appreciate the true relation between Christ's triumphant death and his confirming resurrection.

Throughout this book, we have seen that we were saved by the blood, by the death on the cross. It was the blood on the cross which achieved our salvation, revealed God's nature and won the decisive victory over evil. It was the blood which accomplished our redemption, and reconciliation. It was the blood which satisfied the twin demands of human need and God's nature. And so on.

The New Testament always states that 'Christ died for our sins' and never that 'he rose for our sins': Hebrews 2:14 makes this plain. The resurrection did not earn our salvation; instead, it is the ultimate proof of our salvation. Just as the incarnation was the indispensable requirement for salvation, so the resurrection was the indispensable confirmation of salvation. The resurrection vindicated Jesus, declared

Acts 2:24 ☐
Ephesians 1:20–23 ☐
1 Peter 3:22 ☐
Mark 8:31 ☐
9:31 ☐
10:34 ☐
Luke 24:30–35 ☐
John 10:17–18 ☐
Acts 2:23–24 ☐
Romans 6:1–4 ☐
1 Corinthians 15:1–8 ☐
2 Corinthians 5:15 ☐
1 Thessalonians 4:14 ☐
Revelation 1:18 ☐
Hebrews 2:14 ☐

that he was the Son of God, and revealed that his substitutionary death had won salvation. It was God's way of publicly endorsing Jesus' victory on the cross.

We must never forget, however, that it was really the cross, and not the resurrection, which actually achieved our salvation. This is why the cross, and not the empty tomb or the descending dove, has always been the universal symbol of our Christian faith.

The application of victory

In *The Rule of God*, we see that God's kingdom is both 'now' and 'not yet'. Although the devil was decisively defeated at the cross, he has not yet conceded total defeat; although he was overthrown, he has not been eliminated. He still opposes, tempts, deceives and attacks all Christ's disciples.

The 'now' and 'not yet' paradox of the kingdom means the New Testament promises that we are seated and reigning with Christ, with all the forces of evil under both our feet, *and* it warns that we cannot stand against the opposing spiritual forces without the Lord's strength and armour. It promises that Christ keeps us safe and the evil one cannot touch us, *and* it warns us to watch out for the same evil one who is prowling around seeking to devour us. We see this paradox in Ephesians 1:20–23; 6:10–17; 1 John 5:18 and 1 Peter 5:8.

Ephesians
1:20–23 ☐
6:10–17 ☐
1 John 5:18 ☐
1 Peter 5:8 ☐

The 'now' and 'not yet' paradox means that the kingdom has come, but has not been completed; that the decisive battle has been won, but the enemy has not surrendered; that the strong man has been bound, but his house has not been fully plundered and all his captives liberated; that Goliath has been slain and David has returned to Jerusalem in triumph, but the Israelite foot-soldiers still have to mop up the demoralised Philistine troops.

Some Christians focus too much on the 'now' dynamics of faith, while others are preoccupied with the 'not yet' aspects. We, however, are called to celebrate the decisive breakthrough – and to live in the good of it, and to apply it – whilst always recognising that the kingdom victory will not be complete until the last day.

Christ's atoning death unconditionally guarantees every aspect of salvation for all eternity, but we do not experience every benefit of

SALVATION AND VICTORY

salvation fully and completely now. Romans 8 makes it clear that we are saved in hope, but that hope which is seen is not hope. This means that there simply must be an unseen, unexperienced element to our salvation and Christian experience – that there will always be something for God to complete on the last day. In Romans 8, Paul urges us to hope for what we do not see and to wait for it eagerly with perseverance.

The 'now' and 'not yet' paradox has obvious implications for every aspect of salvation, but we must be careful that we do not make arbitrary distinctions between 'now' and 'not yet'. We enjoy every benefit of salvation 'now', but it is all only a foretaste of what we will enjoy completely and fully at the last day.

For example, because of Christ's victory, our present experience of healing is considerable. Nevertheless, it is essentially incomplete – for not everyone is healed of everything and everyone who is healed eventually dies. Every single healing, however, is both an accurate foretaste and a prophetic foreshadowing of the perfect and total healing of the resurrection.

It is much the same with sanctification and victory. Our present experience is considerable; but no matter how close we live to God we will not reach absolute perfection or ceaseless victory in this life – for, although the devil has been disarmed and defeated, he has not been eliminated. Instead, our ever-increasing sanctification is a wonderful foretaste of our certain eternal perfection, and our every experience of victory is a prophetic pointer to the absolute victory of the last day.

Of course, as well as applying Christ's victory in our own lives by overcoming the devil's attacks, we are also meant to apply his victory by releasing the devils' captives. As we see in *Reaching the Lost*, the church has been commissioned to extend the triumphant rule of God, in the power of the Spirit, by heraldicly proclaiming, demonstrating and incarnating the good news of Jesus Christ.

As we proclaim and live and demonstrate the gospel, we call people to turn from Satan to God, from darkness to light, from idols to the true and living God – we see this, for example, in Acts 26:18; 1 Thessalonians 1:9 and Colossians 1:13.

This shows that every conversion involves a power encounter when the devil is forced to relax his hold on a person' life and so acknowledge the superior power and victory of Christ.

Romans 8 ☐

Acts 26:18 ☐
1 Thessalonians 1:9 ☐
Colossians 1:13 ☐

The completion of victory

As we live in, and grapple with, the 'now' and 'not yet' kingdom paradox, we should always be looking forward to the completion and consummation of Christ's victory at his return.

Psalm 110 is the Old Testament prophecy to which the New Testament most frequently records Jesus referring. The Lord God has told Jesus to sit at his right hand, and he has been seated there, reigning on the throne of heaven, since his Ascension. But Jesus is still waiting for God to make the enemy forces his footstool.

We are the Psalm 110:3 volunteer people who, in the day of the Lord's power, are spreading the rod of his strength in the nations in the midst of his enemies. But we are still waiting for the Psalm 110:5–7 day of wrath and judgement.

On that great and terrible day, every knee will bow to Jesus, every tongue will confess him as Lord, and something awful will happen to the devil and his forces which the Bible likens to death being thrown into the lake of fire.

On that day of consummate victory, all evil will be destroyed, all death will be ended, and the Son will hand the kingdom back to the Father. The 'not yet' will finally be 'now' – for all eternity. We read about this in 1 Corinthians 15:24–28; Philippians 2:9–11 and Revelation 20:10, 14.

LIVING IN VICTORY

The Greek verb *katargeo* is often translated as 'to destroy' or 'to abolish', and is used in Hebrews 2:14; Romans 6:6 and 2 Timothy 1:10 with reference to the devil, the flesh and death itself.

In *Reaching the Lost*, we see that the verb *apollumi*, 'to lose' or 'to perish' refers to 'a loss of well being' rather than 'a loss of being' – to ruin rather than extinction: it is exactly the same with *katargeo*.

Katargeo means 'to make ineffective or barren' and was the verb used in the first century Greek world to describe barren land and unproductive fruit trees. They still existed, they had not been destroyed, but they had been cut down and were quite barren.

When, therefore, the New Testament applies *katargeo* to the devil, the flesh and death, it is not suggesting that they were completely 'destroyed' at the cross. The devil is still active; the flesh continues to assert itself in our lives; death keeps on operating: they still exist, but they were cut down and broken on the cross.

This means that the decisive victory of Christ did not abolish the devil, the flesh and death, it simply rendered them ineffective – it stripped them of their power.

Living in victory, therefore, means living in the knowledge that Satan still exists, but that his power has been fundamentally broken; that the flesh still makes all manner of suggestions to us, but that these are essentially empty threats; that death still rears its ugly head, but that there is nothing to fear any more.

1 John 3:8 shows that the Son was sent by the Father to confront and defeat Satan, and to undo the damage which he had directly inflicted or indirectly caused. The New Testament refers to many different aspects of Christ's saving victory, but it particularly emphasises our triumphant freedom from the law, the flesh, the world and death itself.

1 John 3:8 ☐

Freedom from the law

In Romans 6:14; 10:4; Galatians 3:13, 23 and 5:18, the apostle Paul teaches that we have been released from the bondage of the law by Christ's victory on the cross.

Romans 6:14 ☐
10:4 ☐
Galatians 3:13 ☐
3:23 ☐
5:18 ☐

The law condemned our disobedience, and so brought us under its 'curse' or judgement. But Christ's death released us from the law's curse because he became a curse for us. As we see in *The Rule of God*, this means that Christ was the fulfilment or completion of the law, and it no longer enslaves us by its condemnation.

Romans 8:1–4 explains that we are not condemned when we are in Christ, for God has condemned our sins in Christ. This passage shows that God did this *so that* the righteous requirements of the law could be fully met in us; and it demonstrates that the cross released us from the law's condemnation *so that* we would be released into a life of walking in obedience to the Holy Spirit.

Romans 8:1–4 ☐

Freedom from the flesh

We have seen in *Reaching the Lost* that 'the flesh', *sarx*, represents people in their earthly origin, natural weakness and alienation from God, and that it is often the cause of sinful activity. We see this, for example, in Romans 3:20; 7; 1 Corinthians 1:29; 2 Corinthians 10:3; Galatians 1:16 and 5:16–19.

The basic characteristic of human 'flesh' is self-centredness, and Galatians 5:16–21 lists some of the consequences of the flesh's natural appetites. Jesus spoke about the freedom he brings in John 8:34–36, and Romans 6:6 show that our freedom from the fallen, selfish nature of the flesh comes from the cross.

It is important to note that Galatians 5:16–25 describes freedom from the flesh in terms of walking in the Spirit. Once again, our ongoing experience of Christ's victory is demonstrated by our walk in-and-with the Spirit. Our partnership with the Spirit is our experience of victory.

Freedom from the world

We can say that the 'flesh' is the devil's basic hold inside us, and that the 'world' is his basic means of pressuring us from outside. In this context, 'the world' means the godless society which is hostile to the church and which continually attempts to compromise its holy values.

1 John 2:15–16; John 16:33 and 1 John 5:4–5 illustrate the incompatibility of loving the world and loving the Father. They show that the world is characterised by selfish desires, superficial judgements and sinful materialism, that Jesus overcame the world, and that – through him – we can be overcomers too.

When Jesus claimed that he had triumphed over the world, he meant that he had rejected its distorted values and maintained his godly perspective on people and material objects. When we believe in Jesus, we share his victory over the world by sharing his eternal values. And Romans 12:1–2 and Galatians 6:14 show that living in Christ's victory

This means that Christ's victory over the law, and our resultant freedom from the law, is demonstrated or evidenced by our walk in-and-with the Spirit. Quite simply, our life in the Spirit is our ongoing experience of Christ's victory.

over the world means not being conformed to its values and being progressively transformed by our renewed mind's grasp of God's will.

Nothing reveals God's nature more clearly than the cross. It is through the cross that the world has been crucified to us, and we to the world, so that we are released from its bondage to live in the freedom of God's will and values.

Freedom from death

Hebrews 2:14–15 teaches that Jesus has released us from the fear of death because, by his death, he has 'destroyed' (or, better, 'made ineffective') the one who holds the power of death.

Because sin is the 'sting' of death, the primary reason why death is painful and unpleasant, Jesus dealt with death by dealing with sin. It was sin which caused death in the first place, and which continues to cause humanity to face divine judgement after death – and this sinful root is the essential reason for the universal human fear of death.

Christ, however, has died for our sins and has taken them away. His victory over sin means that we are released from the fear of sin and judgement, and, therefore, from the fear of death.

In 1 Corinthians 15:54–57, the apostle Paul likens death both to a scorpion whose sting has been drawn and to a military conqueror whose power has been broken. Now that we have been forgiven through the death on the cross, death cannot harm us: through our Lord Jesus Christ, God has given us victory over the fear of death.

Of course, like the devil, death still remains: it has been neutralised, not eliminated. It still exists, but has lost its power to harm and terrify. John 11:25–26 records Jesus' great promise to his disciples about death: this does not mean that we will escape physical death, but that it will simply be a transition from life on earth to fullness of life.

THE VICTORIOUS CHRIST

The book of Revelation announces Christ's victory more loudly and clearly than any other part of Scripture. The New Testament uses the

Greek word group for victory (*nike*, *nikos* and *nikao*, 'victory' and 'to conquer' or 'to overcome') 29 times, and 13 of these occur in Revelation.

We see this, for example, Matthew 12:20; John 16:33; Romans 12:21; 1 Corinthians 15:54–57; 1 John 2:13–14; 4:4; 5:4–5; Revelation 2:7, 11, 17, 26; 3:5, 12, 21; 6:2; 11:7; 12:11; 13:7; 15:2; 17:14; 21:7.

It seems Revelation was written sometime in the last two decades of the first century, during the reign of Domitian, when the early church was being systematically opposed and persecuted by the Roman authorities – mainly because it refused to worship the emperor.

In the book of Revelation, the Spirit, through the apostle John, parts the curtain which hides the unseen world of spiritual reality and enables us to see what is going on beyond the earthly scene.

It reveals that the conflict between the church and the world is simply the visible expression of the invisible struggle between the Christ and the Satan, the Lamb and the dragon, the Seed of the woman and the serpent, and so on.

Revelation portrays this conflict in a series of dramatic visions which Christians variously interpret as depicting:

- *only John's immediate era*
- *all of church history*
- *just the years which immediately precede Christ's return*

Furthermore, some people interpret Revelation's series of dramatic visions sequentially, while others consider them to be complementary revelations which present the same events from different viewpoints.

But no matter how we interpret Revelation, we should be able to recognise it teaches that:

- *invisible spiritual conflict is always reflected in the visible physical world*
- *Christ is victorious in every aspect of the battle*
- *therefore, we too should be victorious*

Almost every reference to Christ in the book of Revelation portrays him as victorious. For example:

- the book begins with references to his triumph in 1:5 and 1:17–18
- the seven letters to Christ's churches on earth, in 2:1–3:22, all end with a specific promise to those who overcome
- 4:1–7:17 focuses on Christ on the throne in heaven: he is the Lion and the Lamb who rules and triumphs through self-sacrifice – this is especially clear in 5:5 and 5:9
- the climactic events portrayed in 8:1–11:19 (war, famine, plague, martyrdom, earthquakes, environmental disaster) are all seen to be under the full control of the Lamb, who is already reigning and whose perfect kingdom will soon be completed

Chapter 12 seems to be the pivot of Revelation, and seems to review the conflict between the Seed and the serpent. The victory described in verse 9 must be the cross, because the people in verse 11 overcome the dragon by the blood of the Lamb.

At this point in the vision, the devil has been defeated and dethroned (made ineffective but not destroyed). This, however, does not end his activities; rather, his rage at his impending doom causes him to double his efforts.

This underlines what we have seen throughout the New Testament: the decisive victory has been won on the cross, but conflict still continues.

The three monsters

Revelation then describes three allies who assist the stricken dragon.

In 13:1–10, the dragon delegates his power, throne and sovereignty to a first monster, which then blasphemes against God, violently opposes the saints, temporarily conquers them, and is worshipped by all but the Lamb's followers.

This first monster seems to symbolise authorities who *persecute* the church. We can say that this sort of 'monster' was seen in John's day in the Roman empire, that 'it' has re-appeared throughout history in regimes of every political hue which have opposed the church and demanded the undivided devotion of their people; that 'it' can be seen in some parts of the world today; and that 'it' will undoubtedly be even more active in the Last Days before Christ's return.

> Revelation
> 13:11–18 ☐

The second monster is described in 13:11–18, seems to be an accomplice of the first monster. It promotes the worship of false gods, performs false signs and sets out to deceive. It forces people to worship the image of the first monster and to wear its mark.

In John's day, this monster would have symbolised those who promoted the worship of the Emperor Domitian. Again, we can say that 'it' has reappeared throughout history in every false religion and ungodly ideology which *deceives* people into worshipping anything other than the true and living God. We can be sure that 'it' will manifest itself even more clearly in the future.

> Revelation
> 14:1–5 ☐
> 15:1–4 ☐
> 16:4–7 ☐
> 17:3 ☐

The third monster appears in 17:3 – after the Lamb's final victory has been confidently forecast and celebrated again in 14:1–5; 15:1–4 and 16:4–7. This monster's weapon seems to be *seduction* rather than *persecution* or *deception*, and it aims to entrap people through immorality and materialism.

> Revelation 17:14 ☐

This monster's seductive activities are described throughout chapters 17 and 18, and it makes war against the Lamb by embroiling his followers in immorality and materialism. 17:14 makes it clear that the Lamb will fully overcome this monster.

In John's day, this monster would have been seen in the Roman empire's moral corruption, and in the moral decay which led to its collapse. Since then, 'it' has go on trying to paralyse the church through immoral attitudes and rampant materialism. Once again, we can be sure that it will redouble its efforts as the day of its ultimate demise draws near.

> Revelation
> 19:11–16 ☐

Chapters 18 and 19 describe the fall of the third monster – and reveal that this is only right and just. Jesus the Victor appears in 19:11–16 to judge and make war, and the last three chapters of Revelation describe the final destruction of Satan and death, and the creation of the new heaven and new earth where God establishes his perfect rule.

Being a victor

The central message of Revelation is clear: Jesus has defeated Satan on the cross, and will one day eliminate him altogether. It is only against the backdrop of these two absolute certainties that Revelation can encourage believers to confront Satan's continuing activities of persecution, deception and seduction.

SALVATION AND VICTORY

The Holy Spirit, through the Revelation of John, urges us to be overcomers, to enter into Christ's victory on the cross and triumph over the devil's power. And the New Testament suggests that there are two simple ways of becoming a victor and living in victory.

First, 1 Peter 5:8–9 and James 4:7 urge us to resist the devil, to stand firm against him in faith. We have nothing to fear because he has been defeated at the cross. When we are equipped with the Ephesians 6:10–17 armour of God, we can stand against him and prevail.

1 Peter 5:8–9 ☐
James 4:7 ☐
Ephesians 6:10–17 ☐

We are not to flee from the devils' monsters of persecution, deception and seduction; we are to resist them *in the name of Jesus the Victor* so that the devil flees from us as he flees from Jesus.

In fact, we are not just conquerors, for Romans 8:37 describes us as *hupernikao* – 'hyper-conquerors' or 'super-heroes'. Even in times of tribulation, distress, persecution, famine, war, poverty and peril, Paul proclaims that we should be 'more than conquerors' – through him who loved us.

Romans 8:37 ☐

Then, second, Revelation 12:11 shows that we overcome the devil through the blood of the Lamb and *the word of our testimony*. As we see in *Reaching the Lost*, we are called to proclaim, to demonstrate and to incarnate the good news about Jesus Christ. And Acts 26:18 reveals that it is as we witness and minister to Jesus that people turn from Satan to God, that Satan's kingdom retreats and God's advances.

Revelation 12:11 ☐

Acts 26:18 ☐

We must remember that it is only by the cross of Christ that we can triumph over Satan – both in our personal lives and in the church's mission.

We know that we are called to repentant holiness and radical evangelism, to selfless self-sacrifice and patient endurance; but these only have meaning and purpose because the ultimate completion of the Seed's crushing victory over the serpent – which he won when he died on the cross – is now in sight.

PART EIGHT

salvation and new life

In *Reaching the Lost*, we note that the Bible often considers unsaved humanity to be *apololos*, 'lost', and this is the word which Luke 19:10 uses to summarise Jesus' mission: he came to save *apololos*, 'the lost'.

Apololos is derived from the Greek verb *apollumi* which means 'to ruin fully', or 'to spoil totally', or 'to lose completely'. Although some versions of the Bible translate *apollumi* as 'kill', it really means 'a loss of well-being', not 'a loss of being': it signifies devastation and ruin rather than extinction and death.

Humanity's fundamental 'lostness' is one of the key reasons for God's saving ministry of reconciliation. Men and women who are totally lost urgently need to be found, and then to be brought back to God (where they rightfully belong) and fully reconciled with him.

Although 'lostness' is the principle biblical picture of fallen humanity, it is not the only image. The Scriptures use a kaleidoscopic array of words, metaphors, similes and images in their inspired attempt to reveal the fullness of God's gracious salvation. And the ideas of fallen humanity's essential 'deadness' and 'blindness' are secondary threads which run through the Bible. The dead and the blind do not only need

Luke 19:10 ☐

to be found and reconciled; they also need to be given new life and new light by the source of all life and all light. They need the saving life and light of God *as well as* forgiveness, reconciliation, victory and so on.

We have already seen the saving grace of God at work in Christ's acts of atonement, revelation and victory, but – if it is possible – divine grace is even clearer in Christ's act of giving new life.

Although we may know that God takes the initiative in reaching the lost, the suspicion seems to lurk within some found-and-reconciled men and women that they participated in the process of reconciliation – even if only by calling for help and stretching out a hand.

But people who are dead can do nothing to help themselves. They cannot cry for help; they cannot resuscitate themselves; they cannot even stretch a limp hand towards God. Instead, they need God to do everything for them.

They need the Jesus who came as a divine parent to strain for the heavenly birth of a new creation to give them the new life he brought into being through the cross.

They need that aspect of his saving work on the cross which has made eternal life freely available for all; and they need God in his grace to give it to them, to breath his divine Spirit into their dead spirit, to place his divine seed into their innermost being.

This 'reproductory' aspect of salvation should be the final, convincing proof that salvation is all-God and that it is only-God. Quite simply, as far as the Bible is concerned, we have either been saved by grace, or we have not been saved at all.

NEW BIRTH

Most believers are familiar with the expressions 'new birth' and 'born again', but few think deeply about these ideas or try to understand them in their biblical contexts.

Every aspect of salvation is foreshadowed in Isaiah's four servant songs; and Isaiah 53:10–11 promises that, on the day of his death, when the servant is stricken for the transgressions of God's people, he

Isaiah 53:10–11

will see 'his seed' and 'the travail of his soul'. Some translations accurately render this as 'his offspring'.

Because the Bible shows that Jesus was this 'suffering servant', we can expect the Gospels to describe him seeing his offspring, the travail of his soul, on the day of death. And they do record that, after six hours on the cross of what we can consider 'spiritual childbirth', Jesus was in a similar condition to a woman in labour – he was panting like the deer in Psalm 42:1–2.

John 19:28–30 reports Jesus' *cry of thirst*, which fulfilled Psalms 22:15 and 42:1 (when the soldiers responded, they fulfilled Psalm 69:21) and his *cry of triumphant delight*. As Jesus died 'in labour', he cried 'I've done it!' because, like the Isaiah 53:10 servant, he had prophetically glimpsed his seed, his offspring, the fruit of his sacrifice – a new creation, redeemed humanity, born again in the nature of God.

In John 12:23–33, Jesus predicted several aspects of his saving death on the cross. He explained that his death would reveal God's glory, that it would cause the evil ruler of the world to be cast out, and that *it would marvellously reproduce his own life and nature*.

In this important prophetic passage, Jesus implicitly promised that his death on the cross would bring about the birth of a great host of people who reproduced his nature – in exactly the same way that a grain of wheat falls to the ground and dies to reproduce itself and its nature.

Psalm 42:1-2 ☐
John 19:28–30 ☐
Psalm 22:15 ☐
69:21 ☐

John 12:23–33 ☐

Old Testament background

Every aspect of the cross that we have considered has been foreshadowed in the Old Testament, and it is no different with the idea of new birth.

Passages like Exodus 4:22; Deuteronomy 32:6 and Hosea 11:1 show that the whole people of Israel was together considered to be God's first-born child. And passages like 2 Samuel 7:14; Psalm 2:7 and 89:27 reveal that the people understood their king to be a special son of God.

Some leaders argue that these groups of passages refer more to 'covenant choice' than 'spiritual reproduction', but these ideas cannot be separated. As we have seen, every aspect of salvation is linked with God's covenant, and the promise of new life and reproduction is at the heart of all biblical covenants. God's covenant with Abram guaranteed

Exodus 4:22 ☐
Deuteronomy 32:6 ☐
Hosea 11:1 ☐
2 Samuel 7:14 ☐
Psalm 2:7 ☐
89:27 ☐

a host of descendants; his covenant with Moses guaranteed a people, his covenant with David guaranteed a family line; and his new covenant with humanity guaranteed himself a host of descendants, a holy people, a divine family. This suggests that God provides new life and new birth whenever he acts in covenant.

> Psalm 2

Psalm 2 is especially significant: it points to God's messianic covenant in verses 2 and 6–9, and links the idea of God 'anointing' with God 'begetting'. (The Old English word 'beget' means 'procreate' and refers to the specifically male part of reproduction – the giving of a seed – rather than to the entire reproductive process.)

The link in Psalm 2 between 'anointing' and 'begetting', the giving of God's Spirit and the giving of God's Seed, suggests that the One whom God 'begets' is the One whom God 'anoints' with his Spirit. The association with the messianic covenant promises suggests that this 'begetting and anointing' is part of God's covenant activity.

At one level, Psalm 2 is a trinitarian insight which is fulfilled in Jesus: he is the Son of David, God's only begotten Son, the Seed of Genesis 3, the *Christos* – the One who is anointed with the Spirit.

> John 3:1–21
> 1 John 2:20–29

At a deeper level, however, Psalm 2 foreshadows the link between the gift of the Spirit and the gift of new life which Jesus reveals in John 3, releases at the cross, and which is re-affirmed in 1 John 2:20–29.

JESUS AND NICODEMUS

> Titus 3:5
> 1 Peter 1:22–2:3
> 1 John 3:9
> John 2:23–25
> 3:3

Although the idea of 'new life' or 'new birth' is referred to in New Testament passages like Titus 3:5; 1 Peter 1:22–2:3 and 1 John 3:9, it is most clearly described by Jesus in the famous nocturnal conversation with Nicodemus, which is recorded in John 3:1–21.

Nicodemus seems to be one of the people mentioned in John 2:23–25 who believed in Jesus because of the signs that they had seen: the 'we' in 3:2 suggests that Nicodemus may have been their spokesperson.

Jesus had responded unfavourably to their faith in 2:24–25, and this is his initial response to Nicodemus: the ruler's approach in 3:3, though well-intentioned, reveals a fundamental misunderstanding about Jesus.

Jesus' response in 3:3 seems to treat Nicodemus' greeting as an implicit question about entering the kingdom of God. Jesus explains to Nicodemus that he has not come from God in the way Nicodemus thinks, but in the unique sense of having descended from God's presence specifically to raise people to God.

Jesus' basic teaching in John 3 is simple. People take human flesh and enter the kingdom of the world when their father begets them and their mother gives birth to them. In the same way, people enter the kingdom of God only when they are begotten and born by God.

Earthly life comes from-and-through our earthly parents; eternal life comes from the heavenly Father, and is birthed through the Son whom the Father has empowered to give new life.

Nicodemus still misunderstood Jesus' teaching, and thought he meant that people needed to experience a second physical birth. Jesus, however, was referring to the time foreshadowed in the Old Testament when men and women would be reborn as God's children.

As Nicodemus could not grasp the idea of spiritual reproduction, of God begetting and giving birth, Jesus went on to explain the matter more fully.

Born of the Spirit

One of the simplest tests of life is to see whether a person is breathing; and, in Jesus' day, the breath/spirit (it is the same word in Hebrew) was thought to be the basic principle of life.

God gave physical life to humanity when he breathed 'the breath/spirit of life' into the man's nostrils in Genesis 2:7. In the same way, physical death occurs when God takes back his breath/spirit – we see this in Genesis 6:3; Job 34:14 and Ecclesiastes 12:7.

Jesus explained to Nicodemus that, just as physical life began when God put his breath/spirit into humanity, so new life begins when God gives his breath/spirit to humanity. Jesus insisted, in 3:5–8, that nobody could enter God's kingdom unless they are 'born of the Spirit' – unless they receive God's breath of life.

As a member of the Sanhedrin, Nicodemus should have recognised much of this, for the giving of the Spirit had been foretold in, for example, Isaiah 32:15; 44:3; Ezekiel 36:25–26 and Joel 2:28–29.

Genesis 2:7 ☐
6:3 ☐
Job 34:14 ☐
Ecclesiastes 12:7 ☐
Isaiah 32:15 ☐
44:3 ☐
Ezekiel 36:25–26 ☐
Joel 2:28–29 ☐

(Jesus' words in John 3 should help us to grasp that 'being born again', 'receiving new life', 'new birth' and 'being born of the Spirit' are different expressions for the same achievement of the cross.)

John 3:6 ☐

In John 3:6, Jesus contrasted the flesh and the Spirit in the same way that he had just contrasted earthly and heavenly birth. This contrast is nothing to do with supposed divisions within human beings, nor is it a contrast between material and spiritual, for 'flesh' here refers to humanity as it is born into the world – and, as such, it possesses something of both the material and the spiritual.

Instead, Jesus' contrast is between people 'as they are' and people 'as they can be' – when they receive new life and are born of the Spirit.

John 3:7–8 ☐

Ecclesiastes 11:5 ☐

In 3:7–8, Jesus made it plain to Nicodemus that there is something very mysterious about being born of the Spirit. He drew on Ecclesiastes 11:5 and used the simile of the wind to show that the mystery does not detract from the reality of the Spirit's action.

Although we can see the effects of the wind, we cannot see the wind which causes the effects. In the same way, we can see those who have been born again, without seeing when or how the Spirit worked in them, and without knowing why one person is born again and another is not.

The lifting up of the Son

John 3:1–16 ☐

In John 3:1–8, Jesus explained that entrance to God's kingdom requires God to give his breath/spirit of life, and that this is something which nobody can accomplish except God. Nicodemus still did not understand, and, in 3:9, he asked Jesus how this could possibly happen.

Jesus assured Nicodemus that he really did know what he was talking about because he had come from above – and insisted that he was the only one qualified to answer the question because nobody else had ever been in heaven.

Although verses 3 and 16 tend to be the best known verses of John 3, verses 14–15 are the key to the chapter, the heart of John's Gospel, and the essence of 'salvation and new life'. In 3:14–15, Jesus explained that new life can come about only through his lifting up on the cross. This means that 'new life', 'new birth', 'being born again', 'being born of the Spirit', and so on, is only possible through the death of the Son.

SALVATION AND NEW LIFE

Verse 14 is the first of three statements in John's Gospel which refer to Jesus being 'lifted up' or 'exalted': the others are recorded in 8:28 and 12:32–34. (We should note that, once again, this particular aspect of salvation is foretold in Isaiah's servant songs – in 52:13.)

The Greek verb *hypsoun*, 'to be lifted up' or 'exalted', is also used in Acts 2:33 and 5:31 to refer to Jesus' ascension; and the parallel Hebrew word, *nasah*, can mean both death and glorification – as in Genesis 40:13, 19. This suggests that Jesus' 'lifting up' begins in his death, is publicly vindicated in his resurrection, and is completed in his ascension.

In 3:15, Jesus told Nicodemus that his lifting up on the cross like Moses' serpent in the wilderness would lead directly to the gift of eternal life to all who believe in him.

In this pivotal passage, Jesus promised Nicodemus that he will give new life, eternal life, everlasting life when he is lifted up and glorified. Clearly, this new life will be the life of the children of God, the life born from above, the life born of the Spirit, the very breath of God himself.

John 8:28 ☐
12:32–34 ☐
Isaiah 52:13 ☐
Acts 2:33 ☐
5:31 ☐
Genesis 40:13 ☐
40:19 ☐

Belief in the Son

Belief is one of the great themes of John's Gospel, and 20:31 states that the Gospel was written with the express purpose of leading people to believe in Jesus *so that* they can have life in his name. This is the reason for 'doubting' Thomas' high profile in John, and for the climax of Thomas' dramatic statement of belief in 20:27–28.

John 20:27–31 ☐

In John 3:15, Jesus told Nicodemus that eternal life comes through belief in him – but we must be clear that this is belief in the One *who is lifted up*. Too many people quote John 3:16 without recognising that it must be understood in the context of verses 14 and 15.

The eternal life which Jesus promises to those who believe is life only for those who believe in the one who was lifted up like Moses' pole in the wilderness. This means that our belief will not lead to new life unless it is based firmly on the cross.

Numbers 21:4–9 recounts how sinful, snake-bitten Israelites, who were sure to die, could be saved from certain death only by looking to the bronze serpent which Moses had made and erected on a pole as God's gracious provision of life in a time of judgement. If people

Numbers 21:4–9 ☐

believed in God's provision, and demonstrated this by looking *at the pole*, they lived; if they did not look, they died from snake-poison.

In the same way, Jesus came from heaven as God's gracious provision in the day of judgement for all those who are dying as a result of the ancient Snake's activity. He too was lifted up on a pole as God's means of life: if people demonstrate their belief in God's gracious provision by looking to the One *on the cross*, they will receive eternal life; but, if they do not look to the cross, they perish.

From John 3:1 to 3:15, Jesus focuses on Nicodemus and on the gift of new life to individual men and women. In 3:16–17, however, Jesus shows that God's gift of new life is for the whole world. He makes it clear that God does not intend to reproduce just a few children in his nature; rather, the saving, reproducing Father wills to give new life to the whole world.

NEW LIFE IN CHRIST

The theme of new life dominates the writings of the apostles John and Paul.

John presents the union between the Father and the Son as the pattern for the believer's life in God, and describes the believer's new life in terms of 'abiding in' or 'being in' Jesus. We see this, for example, in John 6:56; 14:10–24 and 15:1–10.

John 6:56 ☐
14:10–24 ☐
15:1–10 ☐

1 John 2:5–6 ☐
2:24 ☐
2:27–28 ☐
3:6 ☐
3:24 ☐
4:12–13 ☐
4:15–16 ☐
5:20 ☐

John 3:15–16 ☐
6:40 ☐
6:47 ☐
20:31 ☐

1 John 1:2 ☐
2:5 ☐
5:20 ☐

Jesus' picture of the vine, in John 15, vividly expresses the centrality of God's life flowing through the lives of his people. 15:7 make sense only if the life, nature and mind of God are infused into believers.

John makes it plain that the gift of God's life is meant to produce the character and quality of God's own life. Those who abide in Christ are obliged to walk as Christ walked and to live as Christ lived: we see this in 1 John 2:5–6, 24, 27–28; 3:6, 24; 4:12–13, 15–16 and 5:20.

The 'eternal life' which John describes in 3:15–16; 6:40, 47; 20:31; 1 John 1:2; 2:5 and 5:20 does point to a spiritual existence in God's presence after physical death, which is received in advance by faith in the One on the cross – but it does not refer *only* to this.

SALVATION AND NEW LIFE

Eternal life for John is *also* a present reality (or else his teaching about abiding in Christ makes no sense at all). It is a new manner of present existence which means that those who believe in the One who is lifted up can share a quality of life *on earth* which possesses all the characteristics of God's own heavenly life.

The apostle Paul uses words rather differently to John. When he refers to 'eternal life' – as in Romans 2:7; 5:21; 6:22 and Galatians 6:8 – he is referring only to the future inheritance of believers. This does not mean that Paul rejects the idea of eternal life being personally experienced in the present, it is just that he uses a host of different expressions to describe the believer's new life on earth.

Romans 2:7 ☐
5:21 ☐
6:22 ☐
Galatians 6:8 ☐

For example, Paul refers to our new life as:

- *union with Christ*
- *in Christ*
- *in the Spirit*
- *Christ in us*
- *the Spirit in us*
- *into Christ*
- *putting on Christ*

Paul seems to use these expressions interchangeably, but they all always suggest both a *definite historic act* and a *continuous process*.

No matter which phrase Paul uses to describe 'new life', it always points to a life which was brought into being by God at the cross: it refers to a reproduction of God's nature through the Spirit and through the Son's death. Despite this, all Paul's phrases also always refer to a continuing process of living the new life of God in the world.

We see this throughout salvation: the gifts of forgiveness and reconciliation on the cross are meant to result in lives which are continuously characterised by forgiveness and reconciliation; the complete revelation of God on the cross is meant to lead to lives which keep on revealing God's sacrificial nature; Christ's victory on the cross is meant to result in a life of ongoing victory; so too, God's gift of new life through the cross is meant to lead to lives which are continuously (and ever-increasingly) characterised by God's life.

The gift of new life is not merely a guaranteed 'ticket to heaven' (though it is that), it is also the gift of God's breath which is meant to transform us into God's likeness so that we exhibit God's nature.

Union with Christ's death and life

Most of Paul's images of new life involve an identification with Christ's death as well as an incorporation into his life.

Romans 6 This is particularly clear in Romans 6, where he presents baptism as a symbol and seal of our union with Christ in his death and resurrection. In this chapter, Paul argues that, just as Jesus' death was an historical event, so the incorporation of believers in his death is equally historical.

According to Paul, when Christ died on the cross, all those who were to be united in him also died. This means that we are immediately united with a death which has happened when we put our faith in Christ on the cross. It should be clear that this self-death is necessary before we can participate in the risen life of Christ.

We have seen that Christ's victory on the cross has enabled us to share in his victory. This is only possible, however, because God unites us with Christ in a new kind of life in which sinful flesh no longer has the authority it once had – for it has been crucified to death. This is why Paul urges us in *Romans 6:11* to consider ourselves dead to sin and alive to God – it's the real truth, not a legal fiction.

Although Paul's use of baptism symbolism in Romans 6 points to our union in Christ's death, it focuses more on our union with his risen life.

Jesus' saving death was gloriously vindicated in the historic reality of his resurrection. This revealed that a cosmic transformation occurred on the cross, and that this was now demonstrated by a new risen way of life. Our union with Christ – through the gift of new life – means that we embrace Christ's resurrection way of life, and live it on earth.

In God

When, in *2 Corinthians 5:17*, Paul describes the believer's new life 'in Christ' as a 'new creation', he is referring to the radical change which takes place when someone receives God's new life and believes in the One who is lifted up on the cross.

SALVATION AND NEW LIFE

Paul uses 'in Christ' to express the idea that what happened to Christ affects every believer in him. The 'new creation' happens to a believer because it happened to Christ as a result of the cross: it happens to us because we are united with him by a miracle of grace.

In his letters, Paul uses 'in Christ' extensively to show both that our new life is completely dependent on Christ, and that it is dependent on our union or incorporation with him.

Paul describes every aspect of the Christian life – both individual and corporate – as 'in Christ': our *past redemption*, our *present activities*, and our *future inheritance*. We see this, for example, in Romans 3:23; 8:1, 39; 16:3–12; 1 Corinthians 1:5; 4:10, 15, 17; 15:22; 2 Corinthians 2:17; 5:17; 13:4; Philippians 1:1, 13; 2:1; 4:13; Colossians 2:15; 1 Thessalonians 1:1 and 2:14.

Throughout this *Sword of the Spirit* series, we note that the Bible regards the Christian life as dominated by the Spirit. In Romans 8:9, Paul argues that Christian believers are not in the flesh but in the Spirit, and he identifies the Spirit both as the Spirit of God and as the Spirit of Christ. This demonstrates that, for Paul, 'in the Spirit' and 'in Christ' express the same idea of the believer's new life in God.

As we have seen, the radical change of new life which has been effected in Christ has come about only through the Spirit.

The indwelling God

Paul's understanding of the new life which God reproduces in us is so rich that he complements his major 'in Christ' concept with a lesser 'Christ in us' concept. In the same way, his very common 'in the Spirit' idea is sometimes complemented by 'the Spirit in us'.

Grace is very clear in these ideas: the initiative is obviously outside our control, and another presence takes over. This is Paul's most dynamic image of new life. We see this, for example, in Romans 8:9; 2 Corinthians 13:5; Galatians 2:10; Ephesians 3:17 and Colossians 1:27.

Romans 8 is Paul's classic passage about the indwelling God: 8:9 stresses that new life is the opposite of the old life in the flesh, and that it is the result of the indwelling of the Spirit.

The indwelling Spirit implies a completely new way of living. It suggests that, in some sense, the Spirit actually takes possession of a believer, who then becomes a new temple of the Spirit. According to

Romans 3:23 ☐
8:1 ☐
8:39 ☐
16:3–12 ☐

1 Corinthians 1:5 ☐
4:10–17 ☐
15:22 ☐

2 Corinthians
2:17 ☐
5:17 ☐
13:4 ☐

Philippians 1:1 ☐
1:13 ☐
2:1 ☐
4:13 ☐

Colossians 2:15 ☐

1 Thessalonians
1:1 ☐
2:14 ☐

Romans 8:9 ☐

2 Corinthians
13:5 ☐

Galatians 2:10 ☐

Ephesians 3:17 ☐

Colossians 1:27 ☐

Paul, it is this indwelling presence which guarantees our spiritual position, our new life and our eternal sonship: we see this, for example, in Romans 8:16; 1 Corinthians 3:16; 6:19; 2 Corinthians 1:22; 5:5.

Quite simply, if God does not place his life within us, if he does not put his Spirit within us, we do not have new life – we stay in the flesh, we remain dead and unsaved.

Putting off and putting on

In the New Testament, the discarding of the old life and the embracing of the new is presented as an historical moment which occurred at Calvary, and which we are joined to by grace through faith in the One on the cross: we see this in Colossians 3:9–10. 'Discard and embrace', however, is *also* presented as a continuing process which is itself a characteristic of the new life, and we see this in Colossians 3:12–14.

This is rather like Christ's selfless sacrifice: it may have occurred once-and-for-all on the cross for atonement, but it will always be the essence of the risen life which we share.

Paul writes about putting on Christ in Romans 13:14 and Galatians 3:27. In Romans 13:14, putting on Christ is presented as the opposite of being dominated by the flesh and its desires. It is a new way of life and means living in a way which conforms to Christ's way of living.

In Galatians 3:27, however, Paul again uses the symbolism of baptism to describe new life. It is as though those who are baptised wrap themselves in the new clothes of Christ to enter a new sphere of living.

Paul also uses his 'putting on' metaphor in Romans 13:12, 1 Corinthians 15:53–54 and Ephesians 6:10 to suggest new ways of living. But Ephesians 4:24 is by far his most significant use of the metaphor.

In this passage, Paul is not suggesting that the new man is superimposed on the old, he is demanding a developing transformation which increasingly reproduces the likeness of God in holiness. In the same way, the 'putting on' process in Colossians 3:12–15 involves developing compassion, kindness, meekness, patience and love.

Paul also stresses the importance of putting off the old way of living in Romans 13:12; Ephesians 4:22–31 and Colossians 3:8. Putting off is not a pre-condition for putting on, for that would eliminate grace.

Instead, we can only put off the old once we have embraced the new. It is the gift of God's life which enables us to start putting off the old ways of living and to begin living God's resurrection way of life.

In the midst of all this, in Ephesians 4:30, Paul warns against grieving the Spirit. We must remember that the new life of God is only possible through the indwelling Spirit. And those of us who possess God's new life must be sensitive to the demands of the Spirit in the way that we approach the old ways of living.

Ephesians 4:30 ☐

God's act of salvation, through the death of his Son on the cross, has produced new life, has reproduced God's life in a new creation. But the new life is not an automatic existence, it is a living relationship, a breathing partnership, and we need the continuing help of the Word and the Spirit to enjoy the benefits of God's new life and to develop towards the maturity which God desires.

PART NINE

by grace through faith

Throughout this book, we have taken pains to stress the fundamental biblical teaching that salvation is by grace alone, by God alone, by faith alone. We must, however, always remember that the Bible is much more than an academic treatise on grace and faith.

We need to remember that biblical salvation is always set in the context of the different relationships that God has established with men and women. Salvation by grace through faith is always *relational*, and never merely theoretical!

We have also tried to stress that the message of salvation is not restricted to the New Testament. It should be clear by now that the New Testament assumes and deepens the Old Testament understanding of salvation, and that it makes some parts of it far more explicit (as well as adding much that is better and new!).

For example, the Old Testament conviction that it is God alone who saves – and not humanity – is repeated by Jesus in the link that he makes between salvation and the kingdom. In the Old Testament, God's salvation is received simply *by trust*; and Jesus teaches that God's saving kingdom is also entered simply by trust. In both cases, it is God who saves – not theoretically, in the abstract; but practically, in the concrete historical process.

The Old Testament records many such relational saving acts (like the Exodus), and they always involve a rescue from enemies, a great effort by God, a sense of triumph and wholeness in the people saved, and a vindication of their trust in God.

It is similar in the saving ministry of Jesus – except now the enemies and results are spiritual, and the great divine saving effort is the sacrificial death of God's Son.

An integrated understanding

The New Testament *integrates* the saving ministry of Jesus with God's past saving acts.

It teaches that the coming of Jesus has brought all the Old Testament hopes, longings, expectations, promises and prophecies of salvation into the present experience. It announces that the Messiah, the Christ, the Anointed One has come to fulfil God's purposes. It reveals that God has saved and redeemed his people. It declares that the Son of David has defeated his enemies and now rules on high.

This approach developed the Old Testament's integrated understanding of salvation, which involved:

- *looking back* at what God had done for his people in the past through the Passover in delivering them from slavery and bearing them into a new life in the Promised Land;

- *looking around* at what God was doing in that day and yearning for a greater experience of his salvation in the present. Salvation, for Israel, always included a daily grappling with enemies and hardships in the Promised Land.

- *looking forward* in hope to the day when the Messiah would come and save them fully, finally and completely, and would make everything right and new.

This 'past, present and future' approach to relational salvation is developed throughout the New Testament, and is an approach that we need to grasp more deeply today.

SALVATION IN THE PAST

Believers rightly look back to salvation as a fully accomplished, once-and-for-all, historic past event. We know that it is God alone who *has* delivered us from the grip of death and from the hold of Satan through the sacrificial substitutionary blood of his Son – for we could neither free ourselves from our captors nor pay the price of our guilt.

We know that it is God alone who *has* overcome and healed our estrangement. We were alienated from him by our sin; he was alienated from us by his wrath; and there was nothing that we could do to bridge the gap.

In the atoning death of Christ, however, our sin *has* been removed and God's wrath *has* been satisfied. He can look at us with pleasure and we can look at him without fear. Our sin *has* been forgiven and God *has* been propitiated!

We know that it is God alone who *has* justified us and declared us not guilty. We were responsible for our sin. We were to blame for our rebellion. We were guilty and condemned before God.

But, through the substitutionary, confessional, sin-bearing, mediating death of Jesus – which absorbed and exhausted God's judgement – and through his imputation to us of his own righteousness, God *has* declared us eternally free from all blame and able to live in his presence.

And we know that it is God alone who *has* given us the gift of new life. We were spiritually blind. We were spiritually lifeless. There was nothing that we could do to open our eyes or to resuscitate ourselves. Our situation was hopeless.

But the Son *has* been lifted on high. He *has* travailed to give birth to a new creation. He *has* died like a grain of wheat to reproduce his life. God *has* breathed his breath/spirit into us. We *have* been born again. We *have* been born of the Spirit.

These are all objective *past*, completed, accomplishments of God alone. They are practical, concrete historic events – as real as the Ark and the Exodus and the other great acts of relational salvation which transformed the lives of God's people in the past.

God *has* acted victoriously in his grace against sin, judgement, death and the devil. He *has* been propitiated. We *have* been forgiven. We *have* been justified. We *have* been redeemed. We *have* been reconciled. We *have* been born again into new life. We *have* been saved.

As Christ declared triumphantly on the cross, 'It is finished!'.

SALVATION IN THE PRESENT

But our understanding and experience of biblical, integrated, relational salvation must not stay in the past. God has not only saved us fully and completely in the past, he is also saving us fully and completely in the present.

The New Testament calls this present experience of salvation 'sanctification', which means 'being separated'. Once again, this is deeply rooted in the Old Testament.

God separated the sabbath, the temple, the ceremonial artefacts, the priests, the levites, even the nation. Nobody could be separated by human consecration. The right to separate belonged to God alone; and whatever he separated was called 'holy' – not because it was good or special in itself, but because he had set it apart for his special purposes.

In the same way, the New Testament considers believers as 'separated', as 'holy', as 'sanctified' – not as a reward for being good in themselves, but because God has separated them to serve him alone and his purposes alone. Believers are called to be temples and priests; their lives are to be like useful artefacts and a holy sabbath; and they are to be members of a new nation.

If, however, we have been sanctified to God, we must go on being sanctified by God. We have put on a new man, we have put on Christ, but we must go on putting him on. We have crucified the old nature, but we must go on crucifying it continually – every day.

This present *experiential* aspect of sanctification has traditionally been thought about in three different ways within evangelical Christianity.

- *'Wesleyan' or 'holiness'* thought usually explains sanctification as 'divine love expelling sin', as God's pure love so dominating a believer's heart and life that it expels every wrong attitude and deed, and controls all thoughts, words and actions.

  Wesleyans argue that, after regeneration, believers must, by faith, have a second experience of 'entire sanctification' or 'Christian perfection'. They base this in passages like 1 John 1:7–9; 3:6–9 and 5:18 which, they argue, hold out the hope that we can be saved in the present from all sin.

  1 John 1:7–9 ☐
  3:6–9 ☐
  5:18 ☐

- *Reformed* believers usually explain sanctification in terms of Paul's idea of the strife within self that he sets out in Romans 7:7–25 and Galatians 5:16–26.

  Romans 7:7–25 ☐
  Galatians 5:16–26 ☐

  They suggest that the believer's struggle between the flesh and the spirit is contrary to God's law, but that it continues until death because of the 'now and not yet' dynamic of the kingdom. They teach, however, that there is a progressive displacement of the old nature by the new nature through repentance, faith and obedience.

- *Pentecostals* teach that all Christians should seek and receive a spiritual baptism (promised in Acts 1:5–8) which is subsequent to regeneration.

  Acts 1:5–8 ☐

  They maintain that this 'anointing' with the Holy Spirit is given to provide God's own power to proclaim the gospel *and* to live God's new life with God's holiness.

  Unlike many Wesleyans (and those early Pentecostals who were influenced by the holiness movement) they do not believe that this anointing creates 'automatic sinless perfection', but that it does provide the divine power which makes a deeper experience of God's holiness possible.

  And, unlike some other believers, Pentecostals do not believe that God expects them to struggle on against the flesh in their own strength. Instead, they insist that God, by the Spirit, *enables* them, by faith and the Spirit's anointing, to overcome the attacks of the flesh and the devil, and to live with God's holiness.

We consider the present experience of salvation throughout this *Sword of the Spirit* series, especially in *The Rule of God, Glory in the Church, Living Faith* and *Knowing the Spirit*.

SALVATION IN THE FUTURE

We often stress in this series that the kingdom is 'now, but not yet'. Time and again, we have underlined that Christ is present in the world now by the Spirit, but that he is also yet to come; that death and the devil have been defeated, but that they have not yet been destroyed; that full salvation has been received, but that salvation has not yet been received in full – and so on.

As believers, we should not only look back to the cross in praise and thanksgiving for what God has done; we should not only look to him in the present for what the Spirit is doing in our lives to make us more like Jesus and to share with him in his ministry; we should also look forward to the final day of salvation when Jesus will return, death and the devil will be finally destroyed, every knee shall bow to the Lord of lords and King of kings, and God will establish a new heaven and a new earth.

Not surprisingly, this aspect of relational salvation is also firmly based in the Old Testament. The prophets looked forward to the day when the God who had repeatedly visited his people would finally visit them to judge the wicked, redeem the righteous and purge the earth of evil. They called this 'the Day of the Lord' or 'that Day'.

The New Testament considers that Christ's first coming is the *fulfilment* of this Old Testament hope, and that his second coming will be the *consummation* of this hope. For what the Old Testament anticipates will take place in one day, the New Testament reveals will be accomplished in two days.

The New Testament still looks forward to a great and final day of salvation, and calls it:

- *the day of the Lord* – Acts 2:20; 1 Thessalonians 5:2; 2 Peter 3:10
- *the day of the Lord Jesus* – 1 Corinthians 5:5; 2 Corinthians 1:14
- *the day of our Lord Jesus Christ* – 1 Corinthians 1:8
- *the day of Jesus Christ* – Philippians 1:6
- *the day of Christ* – Philippians 1:10; 2:16
- *the day of God* – 2 Peter 3:12

- *that day* – Matthew 7:22; 24:36; 26:29; Luke 10:12; 2 Thessalonians 1:10; 2 Timothy 1:18

- *the last day* – John 6:39–44; 11:24; 12:48

- *the second coming* – Hebrews 9:28

The New Testament uses several important Greek words to describe and represent this future day of salvation:

Parousia, 'presence' or 'arrival', is used in 1 Corinthians 16:17 and 2 Corinthians 7:7 to designate the visit of a ruler. The same Jesus who ascended to heaven, will again visit the earth in his personal presence at the end of the age, in power and glory, to destroy the antichrist and evil, to raise the righteous dead, and to gather the redeemed. We see this, for example, in Acts 1:11; Matthew 24:3, 27; 2 Thessalonians 2:8; 1 Corinthians 15:23; Matthew 24:31 and 2 Thessalonians 2:1.

His return will be an *apokalypsis*, an 'unveiling' or 'disclosure', when the power and glory which are already his by virtue of his exaltation, will be fully revealed to the world. We see this in Philippians 2:9; Ephesians 1:20–23; Hebrews 1:3; 2:9; 1 Peter 4:13.

And his return will also be an *epiphaneia*, an 'appearing'. It will be clearly visible to all and hidden from none – 2 Thessalonians 2:8; 1 Timothy 6:14; 2 Timothy 4:1, 8; Titus 2:13.

This final day of salvation will be marked by the resurrection of the dead in Christ, the transformation of those alive on earth in Christ, the consummation of the kingdom of God, the final judgement, and the final punishment of the antichrist, the devil and the unsaved – who will be banished forever from the presence and blessings of God.

A new heaven and new earth will emerge from this judgement, and the people of God will dwell on this new earth in redeemed bodies in perfect fellowship with God. At this point, God's work of salvation will finally have been completed; his past, present and future acts of salvation will all have come together in eternity.

We can say that salvation in the future has to do with being with Christ, with sharing his presence, with being ushered into his resurrection life, with receiving our reward and inheritance, with abandoning the final vestiges of sin, with receiving a new resurrection body, and with perfect, eternal, everlasting, face-to-face fellowship with God.

FAITH ALONE

Whenever we consider the sheer magnitude of salvation, we should have to catch our breath with a sense of holy awe and our human unworthiness. How can this ever be possible for a sinner, for us?

In this book, we have focused on the biblical declaration that salvation is by grace alone, by God alone. It is his idea, his initiative, his good will and purpose, his accomplishment. Quite simply, salvation is completely by the grace of God.

But this has never been the full picture of salvation. We have seen that God did not force Adam and Eve to remove their fig leaves and put on the tunics of grace. In his grace, God made the necessary sacrifice, God provided the blood-stained clothes, God held out his hands and offered them to the pair of undeserving sinners – but he did not make them receive them.

Instead, Adam and Eve had to believe with their minds that God's provision was better than their own, and then they had to act on their belief practically by removing their leaves and allowing God to clothe them with his tunics. They were saved by grace alone, but they received their salvation through faith alone.

It was the same with Noah. God did not impose the saving ark upon him; he simply showed Noah the way of salvation, asked him to believe in his provision, and then expected him to act on his belief. Noah was saved by grace, but he was also saved through his faith.

The divine principle runs throughout the Old Testament. God always acted in grace, but he never imposed his salvation upon his people – for he was calling them into a free, mutually respectful, relationship of trusting love.

In grace, God provided the Passover promise, the path through the Red Sea, the 'lifted up' serpent in the wilderness, and so on. But the people always had to believe God and act on their belief: they had to sprinkle the blood on their door-posts to live, to walk between the walls of water to live, to look at the serpent to live, and so on.

This means we can say that Israel was saved entirely by grace, but that they received their salvation entirely by 'acted-on-belief', by faith.

This relationship between grace and faith was the essence of Israel's covenant relationship with God.

So, in the New Testament, Jesus called people to believe in him (we see in *Living Faith* that 'to believe' in simply the verbal form of the noun 'faith'). Jesus the Christ, Jesus the Messiah, was the incarnation of grace; he was God's grace, God's salvation, present in person.

He came in grace to serve and save, but he did not impose his salvation on anyone. He called people to believe in God's saving provision and to act on their belief. We are still saved entirely by grace alone, and we still receive our salvation entirely by faith alone. We are saved 'by his grace through our faith' – and this is the essence of our cross-made, blood covenant relationship with God.

Works and faith

There have always been those who have stressed the 'acted on' element of faith, and have suggested that this is the most important part of salvation.

They have looked at Noah, for example, and have acknowledged his belief in God, but have insisted that he would not have been saved if he had not chopped down the trees, designed and built the ark, assembled the animals, and so on. They suggest that he was saved by grace and activity, by grace and works.

They have looked at the people of Israel, and have acknowledged their belief in God, but have insisted that they would not have been saved if they had not sacrificed the lambs and sprinkled their doors: they argue, again, that Israel was saved by grace and activity.

In the same way, they have insisted (through the ages and in every tradition of the church) that we are saved by God's grace through our works. They maintain that, if we are to receive God's gift of salvation, we must do the works of faith – we must perform religious devotions, avoid sin, care for the needy, give generously, and so on.

This argument is flawed, however, because it ignores Abraham's faith, overlooks the teaching about belief in John's Gospel, and misunderstands the Scriptures' integrated understanding of covenant salvation.

Faith and Abraham

All men and women of faith look to Abraham as the supreme example of faith. The Old Testament people of God knew that they were the children of Abraham; and the New Testament people of God were also revealed to be the sons and daughters of Abraham. Why is this? It is simply because of faith – the believer's most important spiritual characteristic and basic distinguishing mark. Paul makes this completely clear in Romans 4 and Galatians 3.

Genesis 15:6 is one of the most revealing and important verses in the Bible, for it shows *when* Abraham was declared righteous by God and *why* he was declared righteous by God. It was *when* Abraham believed in the Lord and it was *because* he believed in the Lord.

This means that Abraham was saved (was declared righteous before God) when he believed, and that he was saved because he believed. This righteousness was entirely a free gift of God's grace, for Abraham could not earn it – and did not deserve it – because of his sin in Egypt. Abraham simply received God's gift of 'accounted righteousness' through his belief in the Lord.

This gift was not 'perfection' or the 'infusion' of God's righteousness, because Abraham went on to sin with Hagar and to repeat his Egyptian sin in Gerar. And it was not conditional because these later sins did not affect his righteous standing before God.

According to the Bible's integrated understanding of salvation, Genesis 15:6 was the moment when Abraham 'was saved'; but he still had to go on living in his new saved relationship with God, 'being saved', struggling with the flesh and with hardship; and he still had to look forward to the fulfilment of his salvation promises, to the day when he 'would be saved' – which he saw in part on earth in Isaac, but is still waiting for 'the last day' when he will see the full array of his descendants in faith.

It is plain from this that 'works' are part of living the covenant life, part of 'salvation in the present', but that they are not part of 'salvation in the past', and they are not a condition of 'salvation in the future' (though they will be rewarded at the final day).

Through his conversation with Nicodemus, Jesus bids us 'believe' so that we may be saved from perishing and receive eternal life. And John's Gospel was written so that we may 'believe' and have life in

Jesus' name. But, having received saving life by grace alone through faith alone, we are called to keep abiding in that new saved life through faith-filled obedience – not as a condition of receiving salvation in the past, but as a means of enjoying the blessings of salvation both in the present and in the future. We consider this more fully in *Living Faith*.

SAVING FAITH

The Bible makes it clear that faith, that belief, is the only instrument by which we are saved. 'Faith alone' (not 'faith plus this or that') is the only instrument by which we can be linked to Christ and so receive the divine grace of salvation.

At the time of the Reformation in the sixteenth century, God used men like Martin Luther and John Calvin to restore the truth of salvation by faith alone to the church. At that time, there was much thought and discussion about 'saving faith', and a consensus eventually emerged that it contained three essential elements:

- *knowledge*
- *assent*
- *trust*

Knowledge

Saving faith is not mindless; it never occurs in an intellectual vacuum; and it is not ignorance, superstition or credulity. Instead, saving faith has a minimum content of knowledge which must be received, understood and embraced.

We cannot have faith in nothing – there must be an object and content to faith which must be true. Belief on its own is quite meaningless; and even the most strongly held 'sincere' belief is useless unless it is true.

It should be plain that, before we can have a personal relationship with God, we must be aware of him as a person. We must have some intelligible understanding of what or whom we are believing. Before we can believe in God, we must believe that God is who he says he is.

This means that we must believe certain basic, right information about God to be saved. It may not be much, but it must be something. For example, if we are to be saved by faith, we must believe that there is a God who wants and wills and is able to save us by faith.

Even though we do not need a full knowledge of God and salvation to be saved, we must have some factual knowledge which is *correct*. If, for example, we say that we believe in Jesus, but we believe that Jesus was simply a good human teacher who died and remained dead, our belief in this Jesus will not save us because the object of our belief is untrue and lacks the power to save.

The devil tries to ensure that our proclamation of the gospel is either so dry and academic that it lacks the passion to move people, or that it is so based in experience that it leaves the way open for superstition and falsehood. As the church, we are called to struggle against spiritual error, imbalance and heresy as much as we are called to struggle against spiritual deadness and dryness. Truth matters, and nobody can be saved without a factual core to their faith which is true.

Assent

Intellectual assent is the second essential element of saving faith. This involves the firm assurance or deep conviction that a particular proposition is true. We develop this in *Living Faith*, where we show that to be 'firmly persuaded' is the heart of all biblical faith and part of the meaning of the very word 'faith'.

Some people think that there is an intrinsic spiritual value in trying to believe something, but assent must always be assent to truth. It is pointless telling a lame man to believe that he can walk when he cannot walk – that has nothing to do with biblical faith.

Believers, however, do sometimes urge people to believe something which is true – for example, we may press people to believe that Jesus died for their sins. But without their 'firm persuasion' or 'deep assent' there will not be saving faith – no matter how hard they try to believe.

They may want to believe that Jesus died for their sins, they may even try to believe this, but saving faith cannot exist unless they are firmly persuaded that Jesus did die for their sins.

But even full knowledge and firm persuasion are not enough on their own to form saving faith. After all, the devil knows that Jesus is the Son of God; he even assents that Jesus is the Son of God; but he lacks saving faith because he refuses to trust Jesus as Son of God.

Trust

Saving faith begins only when we add our 'will' to our knowledge and our assent, when we stop saying 'No' to God and start saying 'Yes' to him, when we begin to act in some way on our firm persuasion, when we take a first step of trust in God on the basis of our knowledge and assent.

Fallen humanity rejects God; it prefers darkness to light and selfishness to sacrifice; it chooses what it values and rejects what God esteems. Trust, then, involves a change in our values, attitudes and perceptions. Where before we were indifferent to Jesus, now we choose to receive him. Where before we were opposed to God, now we turn towards him with open hearts. Where before we were unaware of our condition before God, now we long for him to transform us.

Some people suggest that we must receive God's new life, that we must be born again, *before* we can exercise saving faith. In *Living Faith*, however, we show that biblical 'living faith' is itself a gift from God by the Spirit. God does not over-ride our free-will and force new life upon us, but he does 'warm our hearts'; he does give us all that we need to help us respond to his grace so that we can receive his grace through faith.

JUSTIFIED BY FAITH

We began this book on salvation by considering the matter from God's point of view. We wondered how he could show his love in forgiving sinners without destroying his holiness, and how he could show his holiness in punishing sin without abandoning his love. We then saw how God resolved the matter by satisfying himself – his love and his justice – on the cross through the blood of his Son.

Now, at the end of the book, we will close by thinking about the matter from our point of view.

On 'the last day' of time, we will all be summoned to appear before the Judge of the whole earth, before the One who is perfectly holy, perfectly just, and who knows everything about us. How will we be able to stand before him? How will anyone be able to stand before him?

God has commanded us to be holy, yet even one sin leaves us short of his standard. Once we have sinned once, we can *never* meet God's requirements – no matter what happens.

In his grace, God may have forgiven the consequences of our sin – covered and removed it – but this does not change the fact that we once sinned. Our sin may have been cast away; we may have been cleansed and purified; but nothing can change the fact that we have fallen short of God's standard.

God may have given us new life; he may have sanctified us; he may go on changing and renewing us; he may even make us perfect some time in the future. But nothing can change what has been, and we must stand before God with the fact of our sin in the past consigning us to judgement.

The single most important question about salvation, then from our point of view, must be 'How can God declare a sinner just?' – for, in his justice, God can declare just only those whom he regards as just.

It should be obvious that we can hope to be declared just only if we possess perfect righteousness. Yet, as all our goodness has been fatally flawed by even one sin, we can only possess perfect righteousness if we receive it from someone who has lived a perfect life, from someone who has faced our temptations but been completely obedient and fully sinless in thought and word and deed, from the man Jesus Christ.

Our only hope of standing before God on the last day is if we can somehow grasp hold of the perfect, sinless righteousness of Christ's life and can be clothed in that righteousness. Ultimately, for us, this is the only thing that matters, the single most important issue to resolve.

The great truth of the gospel, perhaps the greatest truth in the Bible, is the fact that God justifies sinners by faith, that he declares sinners righteous on the basis of Christ's righteousness, that he receives guilty sinners into his presence as if they were perfect and righteous.

Because, in his grace and mercy, God imputes Christ's righteousness to us (and we are trusting only in this for salvation), we are counted righteous. Like Abraham, we are just by imputation – even though we have sinned in Egypt and are likely to repeat our sin elsewhere.

We know and trust that Christ has paid the penalty due to our sin, that he has borne the consequence of our faults and failings, endured the punishment due to our guilt, taken away our sin, and satisfied God's wrath.

But we do not only need a substitute who, through his death, will deal with our sin and shortcomings; we also need a substitute who, through his life, will provide us with his sinlessness and perfection.

The story of Jesus' life is not mere preparation for the cross; he did not spend thirty three pointless years just marking time until the work of salvation on the cross. His whole life was for our salvation. His perfect obedience in life was as vital for our salvation as his perfect obedience in death, for it was this which accrued the righteousness which he now gives to those who believe.

So how will we stand before God on the last day? It is entirely by our faith in the righteousness of Christ – which he holds out to us much as he once held out those blood-stained tunics to Adam.

The question for every member of humanity remains what it has always been since that first moment of grace in the Garden of Eden. Will we trust God's gift of new clothes (which will cover our sin, remove our fear, and equip us for a new task)? Will we stand naked before God and allow him to clothe us with the righteousness of Christ? Will we depend only on him? Or will we cling to our fig leaves – to our own religious ideas and self effort – turn our backs on God's grace, and stay gripped by our fear, guilt and shame?

The wonderful gospel that we are called to proclaim is 'salvation by God's grace alone, through faith in Christ alone'. No other message is God's good news; no other message is the way to new life; and no other message has any eternal effect.

Through the sacrificial life and death of his Son, God has done everything that he can to save the world he loves. He has now entrusted us with the news of this great salvation, and we must do all that we can to pass on the pure biblical message of saving grace and faith to the lost and dying people around us.

ACTIVITIES for individuals and small groups

sin, holiness and forgiveness

What does the parable of the prodigal son teach about God and the way that he forgives you?

....
....

What is the main difference between forgiveness in this parable and God's forgiveness of humanity?

....
....

What is the hardest question that you can ask about salvation? Why is this?

....
....
....
....

SIN

The New Testament uses several Greek words for sin, which each carry slightly different shades of meaning, and help us to understand the subtle and complex nature of sin.

What is the basic idea of sin?

....
....

What English words are used to point to particular aspects of sin – and what do they teach about sin?

....
....
....
....

What has your personal sin got to do with God? How and why does your sin affect God?

....
....
....
....

How can you be considered personally responsible for your sin, if you have inherited your sinful nature from Adam, and have been pressurised and shaped by your family, friends, background and upbringing?

....
....
....
....

HOLINESS

What does the Bible mean when it describes God as 'holy'?

....
....
....

How does the Bible underline God's holiness and his holy inability to co-exist with sin?

....
....
....

When you are thinking and speaking about salvation, why is it so important to understand both the seriousness of human sin and the brightness of God's holiness?

....
....
....
....

FORGIVENESS

Why can we say that forgiveness is a much harder action for God to perform than creation, resurrection or a healing miracle?

....
....
....
....

What stands in the way of salvation? And what must God respect?

....
....
....
....

The Bible suggests that God's forgiveness has three distinct aspects. What are they?

1. ....
....

2. ....
....

3. ....
....

What are the conditions of God's forgiveness? How can you receive his forgiveness?

....
....
....

How should grace affect your attitude to the Father?

....
....
....
....

self-consistency

Although the words 'satisfy' and 'satisfaction' do not appear in the Bible in relation to the cross and salvation, church leaders have always maintained that some sort of 'satisfaction' was necessary before the holy God could forgive sin.

Why do some leaders suggest that Christ's death was the price which Satan demanded for the release of his captives – that Christ died to satisfy the devil's rights?

....

....

What is wrong with this approach?

....

....

Why do some people explain the cross by insisting that the Law needed to be satisfied?

....

....

....

What is wrong with this approach?

....

....

Why do some people explain the cross in terms of satisfying God's 'honour' and 'justice'?

....

....

....

What is wrong with this approach?

....

....

....

GOD HIMSELF

The problem with speaking about satisfying Law, honour, justice, and so on, is we can suggest that God is controlled by something which is exterior to him. It is God himself, in the total fullness (the absolute holiness) of his personal being, who needs to be satisfied – not a particular aspect of God or a code or quality which is outside of him.

What does the Bible mean by God satisfying himself?

....
....
....
....

What do these passages teach you about God's self-consistency?

Deuteronomy 32:16–21; Judges 2:12; 1 Kings 15:30; 21:22; 2 Kings 17:17; 22:17; Psalm 78:58; Jeremiah 32:30–32; Ezekiel 8:17 and Hosea 12:14.

....
....
....
....

Joshua 7:1; 23:16; Judges 3:8; 2 Samuel 24:1; 2 Kings 13:3; Deuteronomy 29:27–28; 2 Kings 22:17; Psalm 79:5; Jeremiah 4:4; 21:12; Exodus 32:10; Jeremiah 44:22; Ezekiel 24:13–14; Psalm 78:38; Isaiah 48:9; Lamentations 3:22; Romans 2:4; 2 Peter 3:9; 2 Kings 23:26; 22:17; Numbers 11:1; Deuteronomy 4:24; 6:15; Psalm 59:13; Ezekiel 22:31; Zephaniah 1:18; Joshua 7:26; Jeremiah 4:4; 21:12; Ezekiel 5:13; 16:42; 21:17.

....
....
....
....

Ezekiel 5:13; 6:12; 7:7–8; 13:15; 20:8, 21; Lamentations 4:11.

....
....
....

The Old Testament makes it clear that God always acts according to his Name, in a manner which is consistent with the totality of his nature – with his holiness. When God acts for the sake of his Name he is not protecting himself from misrepresentation, he is merely being self-consistent. God is compelled by his character to be continually consistent – to satisfy himself.

GOD'S JUST LOVE

What does God's self-consistency, his self-satisfaction, mean for salvation?

....
....
....

What do these verses teach you about God's love and his wrath?

Exodus 34:6–7; Psalm 85:10; Isaiah 45:21; Micah 7:18; Habakkuk 3:2; John 1:14; Romans 3:26; Romans 11:22; Ephesians 2:3–4; 1 John 1:9

....
....
....
....

What are the dangers of trying to mix God's contrasting attributes together? And of stressing one attribute over another?

....
....
....

How do God's love and justice co-exist within him?

....
....

What does the cross teach you about God – especially about his love and justice?

....
....
....

substitution and sacrifice

God must always be true to the whole of himself. He does not act according to one attribute, and then act according to another. He never manifests one attribute at the expense of another – for they are all connected and inter-related. He always expresses the fullness of his character.

How can God simultaneously express both his holy wrath in condemnation and judgement and also his merciful love in compassion and pardon?

....
....
....
....

What do these passages teach you about Christ's death?

Matthew 20:28; John 3:16; 10:17–18; Romans 3:25; 4:25; 8:3, 32; 1 Corinthians 5:7–8; 2 Corinthians 5:18–21; Galatians 1:4; 2:20; Ephesians 5:2, 25; 1 Timothy 2:6; Titus 2:14; Hebrews 9:14, 26; 1 Peter 3:18; 1 John 4:9–10

....
....
....

OLD TESTAMENT SACRIFICES

In what ways does the first sacrifice in Eden point to God's final-and-ultimate sacrifice?

....
....

How do the other sacrifices in Genesis foreshadow the cross?

....
....
....
....

In what ways does the Passover point to the cross?

How do the ritual sacrifices prepare the way for the cross?

What do Isaiah's four songs of the servant teach about your salvation?

What does Leviticus 16 reveal about the atoning process, about reconciliation with God?

What does Isaiah 53 reveal about substitution and sacrifice?

What do these passages teach about Jesus' death?

Matthew 20:28; Mark 10:45; Romans 5:6–8; 14:15; 1 Corinthians 8:11; 15:3; 2 Corinthians 5:14–21; Galatians 3:13; 1 Thessalonians 5:10; 1 Timothy 2:6.

THE SUBSTITUTE

Most objections to the cross are based on wrong ideas about God and Christ; and most misunderstandings about salvation come from wrong ideas about the relationship between the Father and the Son. The idea of substitution rests on the identity of the substitute. Everyone knows that Christ was the substitute, but we need to grasp who it is who died.

What are the most common wrong ideas about the cross?

How can you helpfully correct these wrong ideas?

What do these passages teach about salvation?

Matthew 1:1–23; Mark 14:36; Luke 2:11; John 4:34; 6:38–39; 8:29; 10:18, 30; 14:11; 15:10; 17:4, 21–23; 19:30; 2 Corinthians 5:17–19; Colossians 1:19–20; 2:9; Hebrews 10:7

Why can we say that substitution is at the heart of both sin and salvation?

covenants of grace

During the 'Last Supper', Jesus spoke about 'the blood of the new covenant, which is poured out for many for the forgiveness of sins'. He was asserting that, through the shedding of his blood in death, God was taking the initiative to establish a 'new covenant' or a 'fresh binding agreement' with his people which promised forgiveness.

What can you learn about God's covenants from the first covenant in Genesis 6:18?

....
....
....

What can you learn about God's covenants from the covenant in Genesis 9:9–17?

....
....
....
....

Why and when did God make a covenant with Abram?

....
....
....

What was God promising through the covenant ritual?

....
....
....
....

What does this teach you about Christ's blood?

....
....
....

SALVATION BY GRACE

How did God's covenant with Israel relate to his covenant with Abraham?

What was the purpose of all the old covenants?

THE NEW COVENANT

Because of the old covenants, what do you know about the new covenant without even reading a page of the New Testament?

How does the new covenant relate to the old covenants?

What is different about the new covenant?

What does the new covenant promise?

BLOOD COVENANTS

What part does the blood of Christ play in the new covenant?

....
....
....
....

What do these verses teach about covenant blood?

Ephesians 1:7 ....

1 John 1:7 ....

Romans 5:9 ....

Ephesians 1:7 ....

Hebrews 10:10; 13:12 ....

1 Corinthians 6:19–20 ....

Galatians 3:13 ....

Hebrews 9:15–18 ....

1 Peter 1:18–19 ....

Colossians 2:15 ....

Hebrews 9:27–28 ....

Why can you say that the covenant blood proves and demonstrates that God loves you?

....
....
....

Why can you say that the covenant blood is the final assurance of faith, the guarantee that God is who he is?

....
....
....
....

salvation and atonement

The Old and New Testaments are united in their common record of God's all-grace initiative in saving a people for himself according to his unbreakable covenants. The three great scriptural themes of 'the people of God', 'the salvation of God' and 'the victory of God' are woven from Genesis to Revelation.

What are the main similarities of salvation in both Testament?

....
....
....
....

How does New Testament salvation differ from Old Testament salvation?

....
....
....
....

What are four main reasons why the Father sent the Son into the world?

1. ....
2. ....
3. ....
4. ....

Which of these four aspects of salvation do you most stress? Which do you least stress? And how can you proclaim the full message more clearly?

....
....
....
....

ATONEMENT

Atonement means 'to make at one', and refers to the complete process of bringing those who are estranged into unity. Within the subject of salvation, the process of atonement includes forgiveness, propitiation, redemption, justification, mediation, adoption and reconciliation.

Which aspects of Christ's atonement can be seen in the Day of Atonement in Leviticus 16?

....
....
....
....

Hebrews 9:1–10:39 reveals that the ritual of the Day of Atonement clearly foreshadowed the atoning work of Christ. Suggest six ways in which Christ fulfilled the Day of Atonement.

1. ....

2. ....

3. ....

4. ....

5. ....

6. ....

What does the word propitiation mean? Where does Paul get the word from?

....
....

What do Romans 3:24–25; 1 John 2:1–2; 4:10 teach about propitiation?

....
....
....

Where does grace fit into the idea of propitiation?

....
....
....

What does the word redemption mean? Where did Paul get this word from?

....
....

What do these passages teach about your redemption by God?

Galatians 3:13; 4:5; Ephesians 1:7; Colossians 1:13–14; Titus 2:14; Hebrews 9:15; 1 Peter 1:18
....
....

Mark 10:45; Romans 3:24–25; Galatians 3:13; 4:4–5; Ephesians 1:7; 1 Timothy 2:5–6; Titus 2:14; 1 Peter 1:18–19
....
....

Acts 20:28; 1 Corinthians 6:18–20; 7:23; 2 Peter 2:1; Revelation 1:5–6; 5:9; 14:3–4
....
....

Luke 21:25–28; Ephesians 1:14; 4:30; Romans 8:18–23
....
....

What does the word justification mean? Where does Paul get it from?

....
....

What do these passages teach about your justification?

Romans 3:10, 20, 24..

Romans 3:28..

Romans 5:1...

Romans 5:9...

Romans 8:33..

Galatians 2:16...

Philippians 3:9..

ACTIVITIES FOR INDIVIDUALS AND SMALL GROUPS

What does the word reconciliation mean? Where did Paul get this word from?

....

....

What is the special place of reconciliation within atonement?

....

....

What do these passages teach about your reconciliation?

John 1:12–13; 1 John 3:1–10; Romans 5:1–2; 8:14–17; Galatians 3:26–29; 4:1–7; Ephesians 2:17–18; 3:12; Hebrews 10:19–22; 1 Peter 3:18

....

....

....

Which three important reconciliation principles does 2 Corinthians 5:18–21 teach?

....

....

....

These word-pictures from first-century life are simply 'colloquial' illustrations of overlapping aspects of the atonement. They cannot be fitted together into a neat theory of atonement; they merely provide insights into a mystery, not a complete doctrine.

Nevertheless, all the word-pictures emphasise the same three basic principles of the atonement, of God's process of unification. *What are these principles?*

....

....

....

How would you explain the fullness of atonement to an unbeliever?

....

....

....

....

salvation and revelation

As God is, by definition, utterly self-consistent, all his deeds, words, thoughts and attitudes must conform both to each other and to the totality of his holy character. This means that God's supreme act of salvation *for* the world on the cross must also be God's supreme act of self-revelation *to* the world through the death of his beloved Son.

THE GLORY OF GOD

What does the Bible mean by 'the glory of God'?

....
....
....

How was God's glory seen in the Old Testament?

....
....
....

How was God's glory seen in Jesus' life and ministry?

....
....
....

How was God's glory seen on the cross?

....
....
....

What do Luke 24:26; John 12:20–28; 13:30–32; 17:1 teach about God's glory and the cross?

....
....
....
....

DIVINE JUSTICE, LOVE, WISDOM AND POWER

In what way had God's justice not been startlingly obvious on earth before the cross?

....

....

How does the Old Testament handle this?

....

....

What do Romans 3:21–26; Hebrews 9:15 and 10:4 teach about the cross and God's justice?

....

....

....

How did the cross reveal God's justice?

....

....

In what way had God's love not been startlingly obvious on earth before the cross?

....

....

What do these passages teach about the cross and God's love?

John 3:16; Romans 3:18, 23; 5:6–10; 8:7, 32; 2 Corinthians 9:15; Philippians 2:7–8; 1 John 3:15–20; 4:7–21

....

....

....

....

How did the cross reveal God's love?

....

....

What did the cross reveal about God's wisdom and human wisdom?

What do Romans 11:33–36 and 1 Corinthians 1:17–2:5 teach about God's wisdom?

PERFECT HUMAN GOODNESS

The cross was not only the supreme revelation of God's glory, it was also the perfect example of human goodness. The Father sent the Son as the 'fully-God, fully-human being' not only to reveal his divine self, but also to show humanity the ideal way to live and die.

What does the cross reveal to you about ideal human goodness?

What do these passages teach you about ideal human goodness?

Matthew 20:25–27; Mark 10:41–45; Luke 22:24–27; Matthew 21:1–11; Mark 11:1–11; Luke 19:28–38; John 12:12–16; Mark 12:41–44; Matthew 26:6–13; Mark 14:3–9; John 12:1–16; 13:1–16

How does this ideal affect the way that you live? How should it affect you?

salvation and victory

The New Testament rings with the early church's cries of victory. The early believers knew that they were victorious conquerors, triumphant winners, glorious overcomers. They also knew, however, that they owed their victory completely to the victorious Jesus.

What do Colossians 2:15; Revelation 3:21; 5:5 and 12:11 teach about Jesus' victory?

....

....

The Bible declares that Jesus triumphed decisively over the devil, and disarmed him completely, at the cross; but it also presents a progressive picture of victory which leads towards the decisive moment on the cross, and which also lead on to its final completion.

How does the Old Testament predict Jesus' victory?

....

....

....

In what way are there foretastes of the victory on the cross during Jesus' life and ministry?

....

....

....

....

How did Jesus triumph over Satan on the cross?

....

....

....

....

How did God prove that Jesus had triumphed?

....

....

If Christ defeated Satan on the cross, why are believers still troubled by Satan today?

....
....
....

What do these verses teach about victory?

Ephesians 1:20–23; 6:10–17; 1 John 5:18; 1 Peter 5:8

....
....
....

Which of these verses do you most need to take to heart at the moment? Why is this?

....
....

When and how will the victory on the cross finally be completed?

....
....

LIVING IN VICTORY

Living in victory means living in the knowledge that Satan still exists, but that his power has been fundamentally broken; that the flesh still makes all manner of suggestions, but that these are empty threats; that death still rears its ugly head, but that there is nothing to fear any more.

What, for you, does it mean to be free from the law?

....
....

How are you tempted to still be affected by the law?

....
....

What, for you, does it mean to be free from the flesh?

....
....

ACTIVITIES FOR INDIVIDUALS AND SMALL GROUPS

How are you tempted still to be affected by the flesh?

....
....
....

How, practically, can you live in victory over the flesh?

....
....
....

What, for you, does it mean to be free from the world?

....
....

How are you tempted still to be affected by the world?

....
....
....

How, practically, can you live in victory over the world?

....
....

What, for you, does it mean to be free from the death?

....
....

How are you tempted still to be affected by death?

....
....
....

How, practically, can you live in victory over death?

....
....

salvation and new life

Although believers know that God takes the initiative in salvation, they often think that they have participated in the process by calling for help and stretching out a hand.

But people who were dead could not have anything to help themselves. They could not have cried for help; they could not have resuscitated themselves; they could not have stretched a limp hand towards God. Instead, they needed God to do everything for them. They needed Jesus to give them the new life that he brought into being through the cross.

How does Isaiah 53:10–11 point to the gift of new life through the cross?

....
....
....

How does John 12:23–33 point to the gift of new life through the cross?

....
....
....

Why is Psalm 2, especially verses 2 and 6–9, relevant? How does it point to Jesus' gift of new life?

....
....
....

JESUS AND NICODEMUS

What is Jesus' basic teaching to Nicodemus in John 3?

....
....
....
....

ACTIVITIES FOR INDIVIDUALS AND SMALL GROUPS

Why should Nicodemus have recognised what Jesus was saying?

....

....

Why are verses 14–15 the most important verses in the passage?

....

....

....

....

What are the key truths contained in verse 15?

....

....

....

NEW LIFE IN CHRIST

What do these passages teach you about new life?

John 3:15–16; 6:40, 47; 20:31; 1 John 1:2; 2:5; 5:20

....

....

....

Romans 2:7; 5:21; 6:22; Galatians 6:8

....

....

....

Paul uses at least seven different images to describe new life. List as many as you can.

....

....

....

SALVATION BY GRACE

Most of Paul's images of new life involve an identification with Christ's death as well as an incorporation into his life.

What can you learn from Romans 6 about your new life?

Paul often uses 'in Christ' and 'Christ in us' to express the idea that what happened to Christ affects every believer in him. New life comes to a believer because it came to Christ as a result of the cross: it comes to you because you are united with him by a miracle of grace.

What do these passages teach about your new life?

Romans 3:23; 8:1, 39; 16:3–12; 1 Corinthians 1:5; 4:10, 15, 17; 15:22; 2 Corinthians 2:17; 5:17; 13:4; Philippians 1:1, 13; 2:1; 4:13; Colossians 2:15; 1 Thessalonians 1:1; 2:14.

Romans 8:9, 16; 1 Corinthians 3:16; 6:19; 2 Corinthians 1:22; 5:5; 13:5; Galatians 2:10; Ephesians 3:17; Colossians 1:27

Romans 13:12–14; 1 Corinthians 15:53–54; Galatians 3:27; Ephesians 4:22–31; 6:10; Colossians 3:8–15

by grace through faith

The New Testament integrates the saving ministry of Jesus with God's past saving acts. It teaches that Jesus brought all the Old Testament hopes, longings, expectations, promises and prophecies of salvation into the present. It announces that the Messiah, the Christ, the Anointed One came to fulfil God's purposes. It reveals that God saved and redeemed his people. It declares that the Son of David defeated his enemies and ruled on high. This approach to salvation developed the Old Testament's integrated understanding of salvation.

What was involved in the Old Testament's integrated understanding of salvation?

....
....
....
....
....

What is your personal experience of salvation in the past?

....
....
....
....
....

What is your personal experience of salvation in the present?

....
....
....
....
....

What is your personal expectation of salvation in the future?

....
....
....
....

FAITH ALONE

What, practically, was the place of faith in the different Old Testament examples of salvation?

What does Genesis 15:6 teach about faith and the imputation of righteousness?

Why does this show that salvation is by faith alone?

How does John's Gospel's teaching about belief and receiving life show that salvation is by faith alone?

What place does works have in an integrated understanding of salvation?

SAVING FAITH

The Bible makes it clear that faith, that belief, is the only instrument by which we are saved. 'Faith alone' (not 'faith plus this or that') is the only instrument by which we can be linked to Christ and so receive the divine grace of salvation.

What did you 'know' about God, Jesus and salvation when you first 'believed?

....

....

....

What might be the minimum that someone would need to 'know' to be saved?

....

....

....

How could you help someone 'assent' to what they 'know'?

....

....

....

How did you express your 'trust' when you first believed?

....

....

....

How does God expect people to express their 'trust' when they believe?

....

....

....

How might this understanding of 'saving faith' affect evangelism?

....

....

....

On 'the last day' of time, you will be summoned to appear before the Judge of the whole earth, before the One who is perfectly holy, perfectly just, and who knows everything about you.

How will you be able to stand before him?

....
....
....
....
....

How can God possibly declare a sinner just?

....
....
....
....

Why is 'justification by faith' fundamental to our Christian faith?

....
....
....
....

How does 'justification by faith alone' fit with the idea of 'salvation by grace alone'?

....
....
....

How should this affect your evangelism?

....
....
....
....